CHARLES FOSTER has written widely on travel, philosophy, law, the biology of spiritual experience, and the evolution of altruism and community. A fellow of Green Templeton College, University of Oxford, he holds a doctorate in medical law and ethics from the University of Cambridge and is a qualified veterinarian with a special interest in acupuncture. He is married with six children and lives in Oxford and Exmoor.

Additional Praise for *Being a Beast*

"Gonzo nature writing . . . Extremely entertaining."
—*The New York Review of Books*

"When it comes to wilderness porn, it's going to be very hard to beat *Being a Beast*." —*London Evening Standard*

"*Being a Beast* is a strange kind of masterpiece: the song of a satyr, perhaps, or nature writing as extreme sport. Foster marks out the distance between us and the beasts in a way that helps sharpen their boundaries and ours—and ours are not always where we think." —*Financial Times* (London)

"Extraordinary, hair-raising, and deliberately funny . . . Atrophied senses limit our lived experiences. Be a beast, says Foster, to become a better human." —*Maclean's* (Toronto)

"Foster wants to *be* the wild thing, living as wild things live. In *Being a Beast*, he nearly convinces us that such shape-shifting is possible in the way he lyrically tells his stories—uncensored, intensely descriptive, and often hysterical."
—*Milwaukee Journal Sentinel*

"An embed with the animals . . . Foster's quirky book shows how emulating animals not only helps our understanding of them—it makes us more human." —*People*

"A splendid, vivid contribution to the literature of nature . . . Daringly imaginative . . . There's not an ounce of sentimentality in any of it, but instead good science and hard-nosed thought. Furthermore, Foster has the gift of poetry."
—*Kirkus Reviews* (starred review)

"A fascinating exploration . . . His attempts to actually be a beast make this a different sort of wildlife book. . . . Ultimately, Foster found reciprocity in his unusual and daring immersion in nature, feeling that he now knows the essence of animals' lives and is somehow newly known in return."

—*Booklist* (starred review)

"A highly original attempt to break free from the anthropocentrism that often characterizes nature writing . . . A rich, joyful, and inspiring book." —*The Independent* (London)

"This year's *H Is for Hawk*, the book leaves you feeling that perhaps Helen MacDonald's bestseller might have been improved if she had only tried to fly."

—*World Travel Guide* (London)

"An extraordinary book." —*The Sunday Times* (London)

"Living like an animal in order to write about it sounds like a gimmick. It isn't. Groundbreaking? Definitely."

—*The Scotsman* (Edinburgh)

BEING A BEAST

BEING A BEAST

ADVENTURES ACROSS
THE SPECIES DIVIDE

CHARLES FOSTER

PICADOR
A METROPOLITAN BOOK
HENRY HOLT AND COMPANY
NEW YORK

picadorusa.com • picadorbookroom.tumblr.com
twitter.com/picadorusa • facebook.com/picadorusa

Picador® is a U.S. registered trademark and is used by Macmillan Publishing Group, LLC, under license from Pan Books Limited.

For book club information, please visit facebook.com/picadorbookclub or e-mail marketing@picadorusa.com.

Designed by Meryl Sussman Levavi

The Library of Congress has cataloged the Metropolitan Books edition as follows:

Names: Foster, Charles, 1962– author.
Title: Being a beast : adventures across the species divide / Charles Foster.
Description: First edition. | New York : Metropolitan Books, Henry Holt and Company, 2016. | Includes bibliographical references.
Identifiers: LCCN 2016002869 | ISBN 9781627796330 (hardcover) | ISBN 9781627796347 (e-book)
Subjects: LCSH: Senses and sensation. | Perception in animals. | Animal psychology.
Classification: LCC QP431 .F67 2016 | DDC 612.8—dc23
LC record available at https://lccn.loc.gov/2016002869

Picador Paperback ISBN 978-1-250-13221-5

Our books may be purchased for educational, business, or promotional use. For information on bulk purchases, please contact the Macmillan Corporate and Premium Sales Department at 1-800-221-7945, extension 5442, or write specialmarkets@macmillan.com.

First published by Metropolitan Books, an imprint of Henry Holt and Company, LLC

First Picador Edition: July 2017

10 9 8 7 6 5 4 3 2 1

To my father,
who never came home without roadkill in a plastic bag,
who paid for my formalin and glass eyes,
and whom I love and honor

To ask "What is an animal?"—or, I would add, to read a child a story about a dog or to support animal rights—is inevitably to touch upon how we understand what it means to be us and not them. It is to ask, "What is a human?"

—JONATHAN SAFRAN FOER,
Eating Animals

CONTENTS

BEING A BEAST

PROLOGUE

I want to know what it is like to be a wild thing.

It may be possible to know. Neuroscience helps; so does a bit of philosophy and a lot of the poetry of John Clare. But most of all it involves inching dangerously down the evolutionary tree and into a hole in a Welsh hillside, or under the rocks in a Devon river, and learning about weightlessness, the shape of the wind, boredom, mulch in the nose, and the shudder and crack of dying things.

Nature writing has generally been about humans striding colonially around, describing what they see from six feet above the ground, or about humans pretending that animals wear clothes. This book is an attempt to see the world from the height of naked Welsh badgers, London foxes, Exmoor otters, Oxford swifts, and Scottish and West Country red deer; to learn what it is like to shuffle or swoop through a landscape that is mainly olfactory or auditory rather than visual. It's a sort of literary shamanism, and it has been fantastic fun.

When we walk into a wood, we share its sensory outputs (light, color, smell, sound, and so on) with all the other creatures there. But would any of them recognize our description of the wood? Every organism creates a different world in its brain. It lives in that world. We are surrounded by millions of different worlds. Exploring them is a thrilling neuroscientific and literary challenge.

There has been a good deal of neuroscientific progress: we know, or can guess intelligently from work on parallel species, what goes on in a badger's nose and the olfactory areas of its brain as the badger shuffles through the wood. But the literary adventure has barely begun. It is one thing to describe which areas of a badger's brain light up on a functional MRI scanner as it sniffs a slug. It is quite another to paint a picture of the whole wood as it appears to the badger.

Two sins have beset traditional nature writing: anthropocentrism and anthropomorphism. The anthropocentrists describe the natural world as it appears to humans. Since they are writing books for humans, that's perhaps commercially shrewd. But it is rather dull. The anthropomorphists assume that animals are like humans: they dress them in actual (Beatrix Potter et al.) or metaphorical (Henry Williamson et al.) clothes and give them human sense receptors and cognition.

I have tried to avoid both of those sins, and of course I have failed.

I describe the landscape as perceived by a badger, a fox, an otter, a red deer, and a common swift. I use two methods. First, I immerse myself in the relevant physiological literature and discover what is known from the laboratory about the way these animals function. And second, I immerse myself in their world. When I'm being a badger I live in a hole and eat earthworms. When I'm being an otter I try to catch fish with my teeth.

The challenge in relating the physiology is to avoid being boring and inaccessible. The challenge in saying what it's like to eat earthworms is to avoid being whimsically ridiculous.

Their sensory receptors give animals a hugely bigger palette of colors with which to paint the land than that possessed by any human artist. The intimacy with which animals relate to the land gives them an authority in their painting far greater than can be assumed even by a farmer whose ancestors have turned over every clod since the Neolithic.

This book is structured around the four ancient elements of the world—each of which has a representative animal: Earth (badger, which tunnels into the earth, and red deer, which canters over it); Fire (urban fox: bright lights); Water (otter); and Air (common swift: the ultimate air dweller, which sleeps on the wing, spiraling up with the thermals at night, and rarely lands). The idea is that when you get the four elements mixed up properly, something alchemical happens.

Chapter 1 is a look at the problems with my approach. It tries to deal preemptively with some of them. If you've got no problem, skip it and go straight down the badger sett in chapter 2.

Chapter 2 is about badgers. It is set in the Black Mountains of Wales, where I've spent many weeks, in several seasons. I've spent about six weeks underground, some of it in Wales and some elsewhere, over many years. The chapter (like the others) is a collage, pieced together from all of those times. It deals with a period of a few weeks, and a subsequent return.

It's a long chapter. It introduces many themes, and some further scientific ideas, which are relevant to subsequent chapters—for instance the notion of a landscape constructed from olfactory rather than visual information. Other chapters are shorter than they'd otherwise be because of the length of this one.

Chapter 3 is about otters. They're long-distance wanderers. "Local" for them is far bigger than for the other mammals examined in the book. They undulate along the wrinkles in the land, and to know their journeys is to know how the earth has crumpled. They live immersed in dilute solutions of the world itself. But then so do we, although we don't usually think of it like that. Their and our ancestors came out of the water, and otters went back. The return wasn't complete. This makes them more accessible to me than a fish.

The chapter is set on Exmoor, where I spend much of the year. It ranges widely, as the otters do, but is based around the East Lyn River and the Badgworthy Water, the streams that course into them from the high moor, and the north Devon coast, into which the river disgorges.

Chapter 4 is a look at urban man through the nose, ears, and eyes of a fox. The chapter is set in the East End of London, where I lived for many years. During that time I prowled the streets at night in search of the fox families.

In chapter 5 I am back on Exmoor and up in the Western Highlands of Scotland among red deer.

We see them from our cars and think that we know them better than the crawling, burrowing things. Our mythology both confirms and denies this conceit. Horned gods high-step through our subconscious. They are big and visible, but they are still gods, and they slip off if we catch their eye.

I've spent a lot of my life trying to kill deer. This chapter is another sort of hunt—an attempt to wriggle inside the head, rather than within two hundred yards of the heart.

Chapter 6 is about common swifts, and is set in the air between Oxford and central Africa.

Swifts are air animals as nothing else is. They are as weightless as microscopic jellyfish. I have been obsessed with swifts since I was a young child. A nesting pair scratches three feet above my head as I'm writing in my study in Oxford. The summer screaming parties down our street are at exactly my eye level. I've followed swifts across Europe and into West Africa.

The chapter opens with a set of "facts" that many will

understandably regard as controversial and tendentious. Yes, I know that the evidence for many of these assertions is bitterly contested. But bear with me, and let's see how we go.

By setting myself the subject of swifts, I was setting myself up to fail. It was rather stupid. No words can come close to them. That's some mitigation for the approach I've taken in that chapter.

In the epilogue I look back at my journeys through the five universes. Were they fool's errands? Was I describing anything other than the inside of my own head?

I'd hoped to write a book that had little or nothing of me in it. The hope was naive. It has turned out to be (too much) a book about my own rewilding, my own acknowledgment of my previously unrecognized wildness, and my own lament at the loss of my wildness. I'm sorry.

1. Becoming a Beast

I am a human. At least in the sense that both of my genetic parents were human. This has certain consequences. I cannot, for instance, make children with a fox. I have to come to terms with that.

But species boundaries are, if not illusory, certainly vague and sometimes porous. Ask any evolutionary biologist or shaman.

It is a mere 30 million years—the blink of a lightly lidded eye on an earth whose life has been evolving for 3.4 thousand million years—since badgers and I shared a common ancestor. Go back just 40 million years before that, and I share my entire family album not only with badgers but with herring gulls.

All the animals in this book are pretty close family. That's a fact. If it doesn't seem like that, our feelings are biologically illiterate. They need reeducation.

There are two accounts of creation in the book of Genesis. If you insist on seeing them as blandly historical, they are wholly incompatible with each other. In the first, man was created last. In the second, he was created first. But both tell us enlightening things about our family relations with the animals.

In the first Genesis account, man was created, along with all the terrestrial animals, on the sixth day. That's an intimate sort of shared ancestry. We have the same birthday.

In the second Genesis account, the animals were created specifically to provide companionship for Adam. It was not good for him to be alone. But God's strategy failed: the animals didn't provide company that was quite good enough, and so Eve was created as well. Adam was happy to see her. "At last!" he exclaims. It is an exclamation that we've all either uttered or hope one day to utter. There is a loneliness that a cat cannot assuage. But that doesn't mean that God's plan completely misfired—that animals are utterly hopeless companions. We know that's not true. The market for dog biscuits is vast.

Adam named all the mammals and the birds—so forging a connection with them that went to the root of what both they and he were. His very first words were the names.* We are shaped by the things we say and the labels we give. So Adam was shaped by his interaction with the animals. That interaction, and that shaping, are simple historical facts. We've grown up as a species with animals as our nursery teachers. They taught us to walk, steadying us, hand in hoof, as we tottered. And the names—which implied control—shaped the animals, too. That shaping also is an obvious and often (at least for the animals) disastrous fact. We share with the animals not

---

* Although the first *recorded* words of Adam are in Genesis 2:23, Genesis 2:19–20 says: "Now out of the ground the Lord God had formed every beast of the field and every bird of the heavens and brought them to the man to see what he would call them. And whatever the man called every living creature, that was its name. The man gave names to all livestock and to the birds of the heavens and to every beast of the field. . . ."

only genetic ancestry and an enormous proportion of DNA, but history. We've all been to the same school. It's perhaps not surprising that we know some of the same languages.

A man who talks to his dog is acknowledging the porosity of the boundary between species. He's taken the first and most important step toward becoming a shaman. Until the very recent past, humans weren't satisfied with being Doctor Dolittles. Yes, they spoke to the animals: yes, the animals spoke back. But that wasn't enough. It didn't sufficiently reflect the intimacy of the relationship. And it wasn't sufficiently useful. Sometimes the animals wouldn't give away the dangerous, valuable secrets, such as where the herd would go if the rains didn't come, or why the birds had deserted the mudflats at the north end of the lake. To get that sort of information you had to insist ecstatically on the reality of shared ancestry. You had to dance to the drum around a fire until you were so dehydrated that blood spouted out of your ruptured nasal capillaries, or stand in an icy river and chant until you could feel your soul rising like vomit into your mouth, or eat fly agaric mushrooms and watch yourself floating into the forest canopy. Then you could pass through the thin membrane that separates this world from others, and your species from other species. As you pushed through, in an epiphanic labor, the membrane enveloped you, like the amniotic sac in which you emerged from your human mother. From it you emerged as a wolf or a wildebeest.

These transformations are the subject of some of the earliest human art. In the Upper Paleolithic, when human consciousness seems to have ignited for the first time in the neuronal brushwood left by evolution, men crept into the cold wombs of caves and drew on the walls pictures of theriantropes— animal-human hybrids: men with the heads and hoofs of beasts; beasts with the hands and spears of men.

Religion remained a theriantropic business, even in the

urbanized, systematized schemes of Egypt and Greece. The Greek gods were forever transmuting themselves into animals to spy on the mortals; Egyptian religious art is a collage of human and animal body parts. And in Hinduism, of course, the tradition continues. An icon of the elephant-headed god Ganesha is looking at me as I write this. For millions, the only gods worth worshipping are amphibious ones—gods who can shuttle between worlds. And the worlds are represented by human and animal forms. There seems to be an ancient and earnest need to unite the human and animal worlds.

Children, who have lost less than adults, know this need. They dress up as dogs. They have their faces painted so that they look like tigers. They take teddy bears to bed and want to keep hamsters in their bedroom. Before they go to bed they make their parents read to them about animals who dress and talk like humans. Peter Rabbit and Jemima Puddleduck are the new shamanic theriantropes.

I was no different. I desperately wanted to be closer to animals. Part of this was the conviction that they knew something that I didn't and that I, for unexamined reasons, needed to know.

There was a blackbird in our garden whose yellow and black eye looked *knowing*. It maddened me. He flaunted his knowledge, and hence my ignorance. The winking of that eye was like a glimpse of a pirate's crumpled treasure map. I could see that there was a cross on it, which marked the spot; I could see that what was buried was dazzling and would transform my life if I found it. But I couldn't for the life of me make out where the cross was.

I tried everything I, and everyone I met, could think of. I was a blackbird bore. I sat for hours in the local library, reading every paragraph that mentioned blackbirds and making notes in a school exercise book. I mapped the nests in the area (mostly in suburban hedges) and visited them every day, carrying a stool to stand on. I described minutely in a pillaged hardbacked account book what was going on. I had a drawer in my bedroom full of blackbird egg fragments. I sniffed them in the morning to try to enter the head of a nestling so that I might grow up that day to be more like a blackbird, and in the evening in the hope that I might be born in my dreams as a blackbird. I had several dried blackbird tongues, wrenched with forceps from road casualties, lying on beds of cotton wool in matchboxes. Taxidermy was my other ruling passion: blackbirds with outstretched wings circled above my bed, suspended from the ceiling on lengths of thread; deeply distorted blackbirds squinted down from plywood perches. I had a blackbird brain in formalin by my bedside. I turned the jar around and around in my hand, trying to think myself inside the brain, and often went to sleep still holding it.

It didn't work. The blackbird remained as elusive as ever. Its abiding mysteriousness is one of the greatest bequests of my childhood. If I had thought for a moment that I had understood, it would have been a catastrophe. I might have ended up as an oilman, a banker, or a pimp. An early conviction of mastery or comprehension turns people into monsters. Those mysterious blackbirds continue to rein in my ego, and convince me of the exhilarating inaccessibility of all creatures, including, perhaps particularly, humans.

But that doesn't mean that we can't do better than I did with the blackbirds. We can.

I don't for a moment deny the reality of true shamanic transformation. Indeed I have experienced it: I have a tale about a carrion crow, which is for another time. But it is arduous and, for me, too downright scary for regular use. And it's too weird for its results to be convincing to most. There are plenty of reasons to read a book about being a badger written by someone who has taken hallucinogens in his living room and believed he's become a badger, but a desire for knowledge about badgers or deciduous forests probably isn't among them.

The same is true for the quasi-shamanism of J. A. Baker, whose canonical book *The Peregrine* might be thought to do for one species what I'm trying to do here for five. He pursued his peregrines to the point of assimilation with them. His express purpose was to annihilate himself. "Wherever [the peregrine] goes, this winter, I will follow him. I will share the fear, and the exaltation, and the boredom, of the hunting life. I will follow him till my predatory human shape no longer darkens in terror the shaken kaleidoscope of colour that stains the deep fovea of his brilliant eye. My pagan head shall sink into the winter land, and there be purified."

If Baker is to be believed, it worked. He found himself unconsciously imitating the movements of a hawk, and the pronouns change from *I* to *we*: "We live, in these days in the open, the same ecstatic fearful life."

No one admires Baker more than I do. But his way is not my way. It can't be: I don't have his desperate unhappiness, his desire for self-dissolution, or his conviction that the neck-snapping, baby-disemboweling, achingly wasteful natural world embodies a morality better than anything humans can devise or follow. As a method, dissolution also creates great literary difficulties. If J. A. Baker really disappears, who is left to tell the story? And if he doesn't, why should we take the story seriously? Baker seeks to solve this problem by developing (as Robert Macfarlane observes) a new language: wingless nouns stoop and glide; burrow-dwelling verbs somersault on the edge of the atmosphere; adverbs behave disgracefully. I love the strangeness, but it teaches me more about language than about peregrines. Always we're left with the question: Who's speaking here? A peregrine with a Cambridge education? Or Baker peregrinized? Because we're never quite sure, the method never quite convinces. It's of the nature of poetry that it never quite declares its hand.

Shamanic transformation possibly aside, there will always be a boundary between me and my animals. It's as well to be honest about this and try to delineate it as accurately as possible—at least for the sake of coherence. It might be rather prosaic to be able to say of every passage in the book, "This is Charles Foster writing about an animal," rather than "This might be a mystical utterance from a man-badger," but it's a lot less confusing.

The method, then, is simply to go as close to the frontier as possible and peer over it with whatever instruments are available. This is a process radically different from simply watching. The typical watcher, huddled with his binoculars in a blind, isn't concerned with Anaximander's vertiginous question "What does a falcon see?" let alone with the modern, wider, neurobiological translation of that question: "What sort of world does a falcon construct by processing in its brain the inputs from its sense receptors and construing them in the light of its genetic bequests and its own experience?" These are my questions.

We can get surprisingly close to the frontier at two points. It is there that I have set up my own blinds. These points are physiology and landscape.

Physiology: Because of our close evolutionary cousinhood, I am, at least in terms of the battery of sense receptors we all bear, quite close to most of the animals in this book. And when I'm not, it is generally possible to describe and (roughly) to quantify the differences.

Both mammals like me and birds, for instance, use Golgi tendon organs, Ruffini endings, and muscle spindles to tell them where the various parts of their bodies are in space, and free nerve endings to scream "Horrid!" or "Hot!" I collect and transmit these types of raw sensory data in a way very similar to that of most mammals and birds.

By looking at the distribution and density of the various types of receptors we can work out the type and volume of the inputs to the brain. Look at an oystercatcher stabbing the sand phallically in search of lug worms. On the edge of its bill it has huge numbers of Merkel cells, Herbst corpuscles, Grandry corpuscles, Ruffini endings, and free nerve endings. The stabbing sends shock waves through the wet sand, and the network of receptors notes, like a submarine's sonar, the discontinuities in the returning signal that might indicate the presence of a worm. Some receptors, sensitive to minute vibrations, pick up the scrape of the worm's bristles on the side of its burrow. This is like nothing in human experience so much as sex. One very good argument against circumcision is that it makes you less like an oystercatcher. The inside of the human prepuce has similar concentrations of Merkel cells and other receptors, which are massaged rapturously during sexual intercourse. (the poor glans has little except free nerve endings, often buffeted almost to extinction by decades of self-abuse and the attrition of rough trousers). In terms of the naked intensity of signal, estuarine worm hunting by waders is tectonic. It's like wandering down the food aisles of the supermarket in a state of perpetual tumescence— pushed to the cusp of orgasm when you see the breakfast cereal you're after.

Except that it's not. Everything's in the central processing. Destroy the cerebral cortex of the horniest German porn star and he'd never have another orgasm. It's not true that men's brains are in their trousers. Even the most thoughtless abuser of women only ever has sex in his head. And an oystercatcher only ever feels lug worms in its head.

So that's my problem: the weird transformation of signal into action or sensation. The universe I occupy is a creature of my head. It is wholly unique to me. The process of intimacy is the process of becoming better at inviting others in to have a look around. The sensation of loneliness is the crushing acknowledgment that however good you get at giving such invitations no one will be able to see very much at all.

But we need to keep trying. If we give up with humans, we're wretched misanthropes. If we give up with the natural world we're wretched bypass builders or badger baiters or self-referential urbanites.

There are things we can do. I've read lots of physiology books and tried to paint somatotopic pictures of my animals—pictures that present the body parts as having the size justified by their representation in the brain. Humans come out with huge hands, faces, and genitals, but spindly, wasted torsos. Mice have vast incisors, like the saber-toothed tiger of a caveman's worst nightmare, big feet, and whiskers like garden hose.

We have to be careful about somatotopic pictures: they say nothing about the nature of the processing that goes on, or of the output. They simply say that a lot of hardware is devoted to whiskers—not that a mouse lives in a world that is subjectively dominated by its whiskers. Yet they're a good start.

We can draw cautious parallels with our own responses to particular situations. Yes, it's ultimately in the processing, but there is every reason to suppose that when a fox and I step on a piece of barbed wire we "experience" something similar. The quotation marks are important in the case of the fox. I will return to them shortly, but for the moment I mean simply that pain receptors in the fox's foot and mine fire in a more or less identical way, and send electronic impulses along more or less identical tracts in the peripheral and central nervous systems to be processed by the brain, which in each case sends a message to our muscles saying "Take that foot off the wire"— if indeed a reflex hasn't already achieved that. The brain processing will certainly, in both the fox and me, ingrain the lesson "Don't step on barbed wire, it's not nice"; this will become a part of the experience that we have genuinely shared. It happened to both of us in a neurologically identical way: we both know what stepping on barbed wire is like, in a way that people and animals who have not stepped on barbed wire do not know. I take it that there are many neurological sequences that it is possible meaningfully to say I share with an animal. If a wind blows down the valley in which we are both lying, we both feel it similarly. It may (it will) import different things for us. For the fox its main significance might be that the rabbits are likely to be grazing in the wood by the horse chestnuts; for me its main significance might be that I'm cold and need to pull on another layer. But that doesn't mean that we haven't both felt it. We have. And the differing significance can be deduced by observation.

We humans tend to denigrate our own sensory lives—to assume that all wild things "do" the wild better than we do. I suspect this is because we want to justify to ourselves our own dismally unsensuous urban lives ("I have to live in a centrally heated house and get my food in cans because I couldn't ever live in a tree and catch a squirrel"), and also because it makes a statement about our own supposed cognitive superiority over the animals ("They smell and hear more acutely than I do because I've moved on from such basic brain stem functions. I don't need to smell: I think instead, and that's much more useful"). But in fact we don't do so badly at all. Young children often hear sounds of a frequency greater than 20,000 Hz. That's not so far from a dog (typically up to 40,000 Hz), and much better than a teal (up to 2,000 Hz) and most fish (generally not much above 500 Hz). And we're far better than many small mammals at low frequencies. It's a good reason, were any further reasons needed, not to go to a nightclub. Even our sense of smell, which we normally think of as atrophied by civilization, is surprisingly (for most) intact. And useful. Three quarters of people can detect, out of three worn T-shirts, the one *they've* worn. More than half can find that T-shirt out of ten presented to them. Like it or not, we are multimodal sensory animals, in a reasonable position to know something of what is wafted or beamed or vibrated to our cousins in the fields and woods.

We have, too, a number of advantages. There is the cognitive advantage, which lets us make allowances for our own understanding and our own physiological differences from the animals, and therefore allows us to describe the respects in which we are different and similar. But there are other reasons why a human is better placed to write this book than a meerkat would be. We are good physiological generalists—a result of our omnivorousness: a meerkat would be too olfactorocentric to be a credible author. And we have perspective. When my ancestor on the East African savanna hoisted herself for the first time onto her hind legs, it was a journey of far more than a few feet. It was a journey into a new world. She was immediately a creature whose world was framed not by the top of the grass and the baked mud of the ground, but by the far horizon and the stars. The Genesis account was suddenly true: she had visual dominion over the things that crept and crawled. She saw them in a way that they did not see her: they looked up to her, and she couldn't help looking down on them. She saw the connections of their trails through the bush in a way that they did not. She saw their backs, their contexts, and the patterns of their lives. In some ways she now saw them better than they saw themselves. This was a consequence simply of bipedalism. Her massively expanded cognition (whether it came then or later) multiplied massively the ways in which this was true.

Sophisticated cognition lets you generate and test (in the comfort of your own cave, rather than in the scary world of arrow, horn, and hoof, where you usually get only one chance) many hypotheses, with many variables, about what the wildebeest will do next week. It requires the writing and running of computer programs. We do it all the time: it's called thinking. It means that the human hunter is likely to have a better idea than the wildebeest itself about what the wildebeest will be doing on the following Tuesday. One might even say that a successful spear thrust is prima facie evidence that the hunter knows the animal better than it knows itself. My ancestors were extremely successful hunters.

With cognition (although not merely with raw processing power, as the example of autistic savants shows) comes theory of mind—the ability to think oneself into another's position by a route that is probably different from the what-will-the-wildebeest-do-next-week type of reasoning. Women have more theory of mind than men, which makes them nicer people— less prone to start wars or engage in egocentric monologues at the dinner table.

There's no reason to restrict theory of mind to an ability to put oneself into another's shoes. It involves, too, an ability to put oneself into another's hooves, pads, or fins. Broadly, it is the ability to appreciate the interconnectedness of things—the very thing that brought out the ducking stool and stoked the fires of the medieval witch hunters. It's no surprise that the Church burned far more witches than warlocks, or that witches are more commonly said to have animal "familiars," into whose pelts they can readily slip. Shamanic transformation is the natural corollary of highly developed theory of mind. If you can think your way into the mind of another species, you can think your way into its skin, and ultimately you'll see feathers sprouting from your arms or claws springing from your fingers.

Since the shamans of hunting cultures are crucial to animal finding and animal killing, this will create a conflict within you that can be resolved only by real bereavement and costly ritual. All civilized hunters, bound to their prey by the same theory of mind that makes us empathize with our children, mourn the death. It's dangerous not to do so, says the old wisdom; and the old wisdom is right. The planet, if not its horned gods, will judge our modern ecocide sternly.

I've put down my guns and taken up my tofu, but there

was a time when I crept heavily armed through the woods and over the mountains. African antelopes look resentfully down at my laptop as I type this. Every October I caught the train north to stalk red deer in the northwest highlands of Scotland. I had an armed passion for the roe deer of Somerset and the wildfowl of the Kent salt marshes. My wife used to come out as a rifle rest when I was after rabbits. I bought my daughter a .410 shotgun when she was ten. I whipped in to beagles, rode to foxhounds and staghounds, and had a monthly column in *The Shooting Times.* My name is in gold-embossed game books in some nice country houses. I've been photographed smiling next to mounds of dead wood pigeons in Lincolnshire. I've fished throughout the night for sea trout in pools on Kintyre, and I can still do the Spey cast I learned when chasing spring salmon on the Royal Dee. I sing "Dido, Bendigo" in pubs, using the inflections I heard at the Rydal Hound Show where I first heard it. I still go to the Game Fair, and still stroke walnut stocks lasciviously.

I'm embarrassed by all this and regret a lot of it. It calloused me. Many of the calluses have taken a long time to wear off. But I learned a lot, too. I learned to crawl, and to lie still and silent. I've lain in a stream in Argyllshire for three hours with the water running in through my collar and out through my trousers. I've sat in a wood in Bulgaria watching the horseflies queuing up to bite my hand, and in a river in Namibia where I watched the leeches looping up my ankles en route to my groin. I've started many a day on the marshes with my eyes at a mallard's height above the mud. I know how the shadows from two sycamore branches dance in winter on the Somerset Levels, why the eels leave the River Isle and head across grassland to a rhyne near Isle Abbots, and the difference between the smells of the dung of two roe bucks that live not far from Ilminster.

It gave me back my senses: a man with a gun sees, hears,

smells, and intuits much more than the same man with a bird book and a pair of binoculars. It's as if the death or potential death of an animal flicks on some old, deep switches. Death needs to be in the air for us to be fully alive. Perhaps this is because many hunts, before we started to go with high-velocity weapons after harmless herbivores, carried a serious risk of the hunter dying, and every neuron had to be strained to keep the hunter physically alive. Perhaps it is because death is the one thing that, without any caveats whatever, we will share with the animals; perhaps the first, exhilarating fruit of that perfect reciprocity is an ability to sense the world as the prey does: it sometimes feels as if you've got two nervous systems running ecstatically in parallel—yours and the stalked stag's.

Hunting rolls back the evolutionary and developmental clocks: you get the senses of your ancestors, which are the senses of your children. All children, if they're allowed to, hunt all the time. Mine are constantly tracking, scenting, turning over stones, and being frankly clairvoyant about where the desired animals are. My oldest son is now eight. He's known around us as "Little Tommy Toad-Catcher." If you take him into a previously unvisited field he'll look around for a moment and then walk straight across it—perhaps two hundred yards—and lift up a stone. There will be a toad beneath. Ask him how he does it, and he says "I just know." A few thousand years ago that skill would have either martyred him or made him fat, rich, and respected and given him the wives of his choice. If there's a genetic element to the gift it would have been selected for strongly. And no doubt it was. The gift lies dormant in many an actuary. It was protected by natural selection much more robustly than the ability to read a balance sheet ever has been or will be. And it can be quickly rekindled in even the most hapless corporate drone.

We're hunters. We can go hunting for pieces of animals'

worlds just as we used to go hunting for their pelts—and using exactly the same skills.

But our splendid cognition isn't always helpful in this hunt. It means, for instance, that I get both bored and interested in ways that, presumably, a fox does not.

Foxes often lie up overground during the day, typically rolling between doze and alertness in a sheltered place. For the fox chapter I did that. My foxes were inner-city foxes, and so I lay in a backyard in Bow, foodless and drinkless, urinating and defecating where I was, waiting for the night and treating as hostile the humans in the row houses all around—which wasn't hard.

It was a useful day: it taught me something about being a fox. But most of what went through my mind was not authentically foxy. I was fascinated by the community of ants that wove its life just in front of my face as I lay prone on the flagstones. I couldn't stop trying to work out the relationships and wondering how they communicated. Foxes presumably don't do that. I wondered whether I was smelling turmeric in the *saag aloo* scent that drifted over the fence; a fox would simply note that there was food in that house and think that the garbage can might need checking later. And I was bored—desperate for distraction of almost any kind; a book, a conversation, an intrigue.

Animals do get bored. Or at least relatively bored: a dog in the back of a car would rather be off chasing rabbits. But I doubt that the stress of complete nonevent is quite as debilitating for them as it is for me. Perhaps they never have such stress. Perhaps there is always the perceived possibility of annihilation, sex, or food to give piquancy to their long wakeful days. I, lying in my own dung in London E3, was variously less or more realistic about those possibilities, and it was hell.

I have been dancing around the question of consciousness.

This, of course, is because, like everyone else, I have no idea how to dance with it. In just about every book on animal perception there appears, as a handy epigraph, the line of the American philosopher Thomas Nagel: "What is it like to be a bat?" It's an ironic citation, since Nagel meant to point up the insuperable problems of writing books that purport to say anything about the consciousness of a nonhuman creature. First: we simply don't know, in many cases, whether a particular species has consciousness (or whether particular members of particular species have consciousness—might one not have talking, self-reflective, and nontalking animals, as in the Narnia chronicles?). And second (and this was Nagel's main point): consciousness cannot be said to be "like" anything else, which makes exploration with simile impossible, and exploration with metaphor tricky.

Consciousness is subjectivity: my sense that there is a Charles Foster who is distinct from other beings. And distinct, indeed, from my own body. The Charles Foster that I have a robust conviction that there *is* me in a way that my body is not. Lots of the cells that presently make up my body did not exist last week and will be dead next week, and yet I say today that Charles Foster walked up a hill in Somerset last week and will be in Athens next week. By saying this I really mean that there is some essential *I* that inhabits my body. It sounds suspiciously as if I'm talking about my soul.

No one has the faintest idea about the origins of consciousness. The reductionists insist that it is an artifact of my neurological hardware—a sort of substance secreted by my brain. But no one has ever been able to suggest convincingly how it erupted in the first place or why, when it did, it should have been favored by natural selection.

We can see the fingerprints of consciousness in the human historical record: it seems to have emerged sometime in the

Upper Paleolithic, as evidenced by an explosion of symbolism, by the proliferation of things that shout "I and not you."

It has been convincingly suggested that the induction of altered states of consciousness by ascetic practice, exhaustion, dehydration, or the ingestion of hallucinogenic substances might have been the catalyst of a process of which consciousness was the end product. But that, while interesting, doesn't begin to explain the nature of consciousness, or the reasons for its survival, or its location. T. H. Huxley observed that the emergence of consciousness from electronically irritated nervous tissue is just as mysterious as the genie emerging from the lamp when it was rubbed by Aladdin. Modern neuroscience has nothing to add to that observation.

It's a sickening problem for the reductionist, because no one has any idea what consciousness is for, and nor are there any suggestions of the useful quality of which consciousness might be an incidental by-product. You don't need consciousness for anything on which natural selection can bite. You don't need it to catch food, or to mate. A sense of *I* doesn't increase the incentive to stop your body from being chewed by a predator. Theory of mind might well confer a selective advantage, but you don't need consciousness for theory of mind. We even show visual discrimination without consciousness. Take, for instance, Lawrence Weiskrantz's experiments on a patient who was cortically blind in the left visual field. His eye worked, but the connections to or in the visual cortex of his brain did not. He therefore said that he could not see objects in the left visual field. But when he was required to say what was there, he was much more accurate than chance suggested. If a letter box was vertically aligned, he would tend strongly to orient letters vertically. He was good at mimicking the expression of an "invisible" person in the left visual field. He dealt quite well with a world with which he had no idea he had any relationship at all. The *he* he described to himself didn't impinge on the world of the left visual field. And yet his body did.

Consciousness is certainly present in some animals. It has been convincingly demonstrated in, for instance, New Caledonian crows—often by experiments involving self-recognition. The better we get at looking for consciousness, the more we find it. The earth seems to be a garden good at growing it. But consciousness has not been shown, so far as I know, in any of the species described in this book. I'd be surprised if it were absent—at least in the fox and the badger—but I've not assumed that it is present (as almost all children's and many adults' storybooks about animals do). Even if consciousness had been demonstrated, it couldn't make much difference to this book. Where consciousness is present, as in humans, its workings in even one individual can be explored only by novelists and poets. And the best of them will conclude that the individual is elusive. That's even when, as fellow humans, we've got some limited idea of how consciousness might operate in another human. What might it mean to be a particular conscious fox? That's an enterprise on the wild frontiers of poesy. And if an answer were possible, it might not tell us much about the world of foxes in general.

It's quite interesting enough, and certainly hard enough, to try to say what it's like to be a generic sensate fox.

So much for physiology. I share a lot of physiology with my animals, and what I don't share I can have a reasonable go at probing. The second point at which I meet them is landscape. I can go to where they are. The same rain falls on us; we're pricked by the same gorse; we feel the same shudders through the ground as the juggernauts pass; we see the same farmer walk past carrying the same gun. They mean different things to us, of course. The gun is unlikely to mean death to me; the rain will mean earthworms on the surface, which will be more interesting to a badger than to me. But we still share something real and objective, the badger and I. Yes, our individual worlds are custom-tailored inside our heads by our unique neurological software; yes, it is truly hard to say how a rock on a moor appears to any other creature. But that doesn't mean that the rock doesn't objectively exist, or that the attempt to perceive it through the sense receptors of a nonhuman is doomed to meaninglessness or incoherence.

The animals and I speak a shared language: the language of the buzzing of our neurons. Often they speak in a difficult— though never quite incomprehensible—dialect. When it is difficult to make out what is being said, context helps. The context is always the land.

The animals are made out of the land. Almost every molecule of a typical badger came from somewhere in the area of 150 acres around its birth sett. After being squeezed through its mother's birth canal, deep inside the earth, it enters the dusk of its wood through another tunnel, this time made of earth. It will go back through the same or a similar tunnel at the end. It is likely to die underground, surrounded by the same earth. Its body will be incorporated into the wall of the sett and will be food for worms, which in turn will become parts of the bodies of the next generation or two. You'd expect a deep, fecund resonance between land and animal. And that's what you find. Few animals export well.

I'm much less local. Despite my best efforts, many of my molecules come from China and Thailand. I have to work a lot harder to get any kind of resonance. Yet there are many things that can help: history books, the songs and tunes of dead farmers, the stories that cling to the land and to my mind as earth clings to the back of a badger. I can slowly learn the mythological language in which the land speaks both to me and to the badger, and it suffices for some sort of conversation even if the badger and I falter in our neuronal dialects.

For this, of course, it helps to be an unabashed hippie. Frank Fraser Darling insisted on going barefoot, year-round, on his beloved island, on the basis that it was hard to feel the pulse of the universe through half an inch of Commando sole, and I'm sure that he was an even better zoologist as a result. So off with the kit and on with the instincts. Animals don't wear clothes outside Beatrix Potter and Alison Uttley. Gore-Tex is just another layer standing between you and the way the less heavily furred animals sense the world.

Someone I knew walked naked for hundreds of miles across England. (The English, being English, simply refused to acknowledge that there was anything unusual when they met him, and wished him an uncomplicated "Good morning.") Wet suits are condoms that prevent your imagination from being fertilized by mountain rivers.

Learn old tunes; eat food that comes from where you are. Sit in the corner of a field hearing. Put in wax earplugs, close your eyes, and smell. Sniff everything, wherever you are: turn on those olfactory centers. Say, with Saint Francis, "Hello, Brother Ox," and mean it.

Evolutionary biology is a numinous statement of the interconnectedness of things—a sort of scientific Advaita: feel it as well as know it. Feel it to know it properly.

What's an animal? It's a rolling conversation with the land from which it comes and of which it consists. What's a human? It's a rolling conversation with the land from which it comes and of which it consists—but a more stilted, stammering conversation than that of most wild animals. The conversations can become stories and acquire the shape and taste of personality. Then they become the sort of animals we celebrate, and the sort of people we want to sit next to at dinner.

I want to have a more articulate talk with the land. It's just another way of knowing myself better, and my self-obsession insists that that's worthwhile. A good way to go about it is to have a more articulate talk with the furry, feathered, scaly, whooping, swooping, screaming, soaring, grunting, crushing, panting, flapping, farting, wrenching, waddling, dislocating, loping, ripping, springing, exulting lumps of the land that we call the animals.

You get good at talking by talking. You get good relationships by relating, which takes time. You also need to know some facts about the other party. So I read books about photosynthesis and standing stones and schist and scat and scent. I pasted leaves into my notebooks and stroked them. I bought audiobooks of birdcalls and realized, on the Tube between Paddington and Farringdon, that I could tell a lot about the personality of a bird and the details of its life by hearing the noise it made. Without knowing what it was (since some of those audiobooks blessedly don't ram the species name down your ears), I knew somehow that a whitethroat danced fearfully in deciduous summer shadows, looking for death from above, and picked insects with a beak like the finest surgical forceps, and fluffed and fussed and went south early.

"Pretentious mystical claptrap," boomed my farmer friend Burt, whom we'll meet in the next chapter. Yet it was so. And on the Tube between Farringdon and Paddington I realized that this wasn't at all surprising; that you could give a fair summary of the history and politics of Russia by listening to Russians talk in Russian about shopping and the weather— even if, and perhaps because, you didn't understand a word.

But most of all I hung around. I sat naked and shivering on a moorland, watching the clouds break. I swam into the dark holes of the East Lyn River, where the eels lie. I dug a hole in a Welsh hillside and lived in it. I lay by the side of a big road, outraged by the headlights, feeling the pavement shudder beneath me as the trucks went past. And, like everyone else, I shuffled in an unnecessary coat through the park with the kids on a Sunday afternoon and fed the ducks. And slowly, slowly, I picked up a few words, and knew, too, that my words were heard.

Wittgenstein said that if a lion could speak, we couldn't understand a word it was saying, since the form of a lion's world is so massively different from our own. He was wrong. I know he was wrong.

2. BADGER

When you put a worm into your mouth, it senses the heat as something sinister. You'd have thought it might make a bid for freedom by going down, into the deeper darkness that usually means home and safety, and head for your esophagus. But it doesn't. It goes for the gaps between your teeth. There are plenty in mine. No one had braces in Sheffield in the 1970s. It narrows its body to a thread and urges itself through. If it is frustrated, as it would be by expensive bridgework, it goes into a frenzy: it thrashes, whirling one end like a centrifuge around the middle of its body: it lashes your gums. Eventually, frustrated, it curls up in the moist space next to the frenulum and considers its position. If you open your mouth again it'll be off, pressing its tail against the floor of your mouth like a sprinter pushing off from the blocks.

This is all disgusting. It is a good argument for cremation.

When you bite into a worm for the first time you expect the sort of performance that every angler knows and I hope every angler hates: twisting, questing against the hook. But it doesn't happen. Even if, like me, you can't bring yourself to mash the worm with your molars, and instead nip it genteelly with your incisors, the main action is crushing, and that seems to be different. Crushed animals just lie. It doesn't seem to hurt. When a large piece of Scotland fell off and landed on my arm it didn't hurt a bit. In my case there was the woozy, beatific opiate high as the endorphins pumped around, and the sheer diversion of seeing splintered bone and divided nerves. Perhaps annelid worms have some crude opiate-mediated system. I haven't looked it up, but it seems very unlikely. That would be absurd evolutionary extravagance. Anyway, both ends of the worm capitulate. And then I can move the worm back and chew it.

Earthworms taste of slime and the land. They are the ultimate local food and, as the wine people would say, have a very distinct *terroir*. Worms from Chablis have a long, mineral finish. Worms from Picardy are musty; they taste of decay and splintered wood. Worms from the high Kent Weald are fresh and uncomplicated; they'd appear in the list recommended with a grilled sole. Worms from the Somerset Levels have a stolid, unfashionable taste of leather and stout. But the worms of the Welsh Black Mountains are hard to place: they would be a serious challenge on a blind tasting. I'm not quite pretentious enough to have a go at describing them.

The taste of the body predominates. The slime is different from the body, and its taste is mysteriously variable. It doesn't relate in any obvious way to the *terroir* of the body. You can suck off the slime, and you'll find that Chablis slime, at least in the spring, is lemongrass and pig shit. The slime of the Weald is burning rubber and halitosis.

The tastes vary with the seasons, but not as much as you'd expect. The seasons bring out one element rather than another in the taste: they change the tone. You get more diaper liner than paraffin in Norfolk in August than in January, but they are both there all the time.

About 85 percent of an average badger's diet is earthworms. This fact both drains badgers of some of their charisma and makes them excitingly inaccessible.

Badgers are both the best and the worst place to start. The worst, because we think we know them. Our childhood badger anthropomorphisms are among our most cherished, and even when we're big and unsentimental, they continue to seem plausible. A pipe of herb tobacco would sit comfortably in those massive, undislocatable jaws. Those hams, smoked and lauded by gypsies, designed to lumber thousands of nocturnal miles in search of worms and roots, really would look good in moleskin breeches. The front paws, which are powerful digging and slashing machines, look as if they could undo a brass waistcoat button after a big Sunday roast. Their citadels are often centuries old, implying solidity and wisdom. Their grave striped heads would shake authoritatively when disapproving of the plans of flightier animals.

But they are the best place to start because iconoclasm's easier with a badger than (say) a heron, in which I've invested much less. Going after badgers is the best way to scorch your sentiment. They are great tutors. In the darkening woods they look you shrewdly in the eye, finger their corduroy braces thoughtfully, and then slash open your face.

* * *

For me, badgers meant Burt and the Black Mountains. Not because badgers are obviously linked with mid-Wales: they're not. Somerset, Gloucestershire, or Devon would make more sense. But because Burt has a backhoe.

Burt and I go back a long way. We have bled, suffered, cursed, and caroused together in some of the most unpleasant places on the planet. And now he farms, lisps, and ambles on some of the steepest and least productive land in Britain. Stones and gradient stop money from sprouting in the open fields; ancient, dripping broad-leaved woodland stops it in the valleys. Burt doesn't care. You don't need money for homemade cider, homemade sex, or the view.

He met us at Abergavenny Station. I had my own cub with me: Tom, aged eight. Badgers are highly sociable, familial creatures. A lone badger is unthinkable. And Tom, who is profoundly dyslexic and therefore gifted with a dazzlingly holistic, intimately relational view of the world, is, I'd guess, far closer to being a badger than I am. He doesn't have my disability: the tragic pathology of seeing something as meaningful only if and insofar as I can stuff it into a proposition.

Badgers communicate effectively and copiously, but, everyone supposes, without the burden of abstraction. For that you need the disaster of written language, which makes things something other than they are: turns a root into the word "root" and smothers it with layers of nuance so thick that the thing itself suffocates. Tom still knows what a root is, and always will. So does a badger, which likes eating roots and dislikes eating abstractions. Tom defines "Tom" ecologically, in terms of the nexus of relationships (with other humans and with the whole natural world) in which he exists and of which he consists. This is more accurate than my picture of myself, as well as being healthier, more interesting, and more badgerlike. I doubt there's a lot of morbid atomism in a badger sett. Also, Tom is four and half feet tall. I'm six foot three. His view is quite literally closer to that of a badger than mine. Ferns brush his face as they brush a badger's; his nose is nearer the leaf mold of which he, I, and all badgers will eventually be a part, and which is the staple of earthworms.

We piled into Burt's Land Rover, drove off, drove back to pick up and tie on the rear bumper, went to a pie shop to fill ourselves up with meat from condemned cows (since we weren't looking forward to earthworms), and went to the farm.

It was in Burt's kitchen, years before, that I had first started to reflect seriously on the possibility of being another animal. This was not because he lives as an ontological amphibian, slopping happily between humanness and animality: I have long known that to be the case. It's a lot of his charm. Nor because his kitchen is a continually shifting border between wilderness and *Peppa Pig*. It is because his wife, Meg, is a witch.

In the nicest possible way. She sticks pins into people to help them, rather than into wax models of people to harm them. But she has the same notions of the interconnectedness of things that, in Merrie England, would have sent her up in flames.

Burt is a familiar rather than a husband; a companion from across one of those arbitrary species boundaries—shaggy, lolloping, and happy enough with his leg in a gin trap.

Burt and I met fifteen years ago in the Sahara, on the Marathon des Sables, which he was running in Green Flash tennis shoes. I rubbed iodine into what was left of his feet, and he invited me to his farm.

He was born in this valley, and then lisped his way out to diamond mines in Namibia, to Cambridge, to veterinary clinics in Ethiopia, Afghanistan, and Gaza, and then into Meg's magnificent knickers and the shearing shed.

Their kitchen is a crossing place. The hill bleeds into the carpet. There's a Bronze Age ax head next to the PC. The Tibetan Book of the Dead leans against Jamie Oliver. There's a cauldron of hallucinogenic herbs by the chicken nuggets.

Meg took it for granted that I, or anyone, could be an animal.

"In all civilized cultures people are doing it all the time. The shamans shuttle to and fro between their bodies and the bodies of bears, crows, or whatever. You want to fly? There are dozens of cocktails that will give you wings. There are some recipes there." She gestured to the bookshelf. "You want to be a fox? It just takes a bit of practice in a darkened room with a candle and a chicken. These creatures are, after all, just a few evolutionary years upstream of us. There are boats that can go fast against the stream; I know some of the boatmen. Or, if you're smart, you can reverse the flow."

I didn't doubt it then, and I certainly don't now. Though I wanted it, I feared it. But I didn't fear physiology books or the business of empathy. I wanted to see how far into a badger's skin they could take me.

* * *

I planned to burrow into the side of a flat-topped mountain. On the top of the mountain, men used to kill their children. Badgers don't do that; they know that dogs, trucks, TB, and starvation will harvest whatever the gods need.

Scree falls from the infanticidal sanctuary and then, when the land curves out, grass starts to cling to the stone, and then the grass gives way to desperate clumps of bracken and finally, near the river, to oak, ash, beech, and elder. The elders come for the water, and the badgers come for the elders: they eat the berries the way kids eat potato chips, their shit is knobbly with the seeds, and so the elders and the badgers travel together. You often find badger setts near water, but that's because of the elders; I've never seen badgers drink at a river (although they must), and they've never learned to scoop out fish with those hook-feet of theirs. They seem to get most of their water from the earthworms.

This river rises in a sullen swamp of cotton grass and sphagnum, which doesn't deserve the bubbling enthusiasm of its curlews. It takes the water five miles to start to stutter out the curlews' bubbles. By the time it hits the badger valley the river has learned a lot, and has many voices and much conversation. Many living things, with very different ears, come to listen and to talk. The badgers wouldn't be there otherwise.

Conversational and dietary monoculture are as deadly for them as for us. Badgers can't live on curlews; they eat ecosystems.

There's every reason to suppose that they were in this valley long before the Bronze Age child killers. There are some great badger fortresses here, tangled labyrinths that hollow out the hill so that it would ring like a bodhran if one of the dark gods stamped in disgust at the taste of a child.

The population is ancient and isolated; they won't have had the chatty commerce of lowland badgers. Traveling boars, frustrated in their search for a mate back home, can't have reached this redoubt very often. The DNA went round and round, getting sick and dizzy over the centuries. One of the skulls in a heap of spoil had a weirdly undershot jaw; another a sagittal crest like a cockatoo. Some of the footprints along the badger paths had six or seven toe marks.

The skulls are in the spoil because badgers often die underground, in the midst of their families, and are buried there. Their bodies often cause a new kink in the tunnel. Grandma's body determines the geography of the next few generations. We dump our dead beyond the outer ring road where they won't interfere with the way we live.

* * *

I cheated. I'd thought of enlarging a disused badger sett, but I wasn't confident of persuading the police that I wasn't badger digging, and I didn't like the idea of inhaling, along with the good earth of mid-Wales, a huge dose of TB bacilli. And then there was my wife, who rightly expected any hole I dug to collapse in on Tom, which would have created lots of paperwork. The backhoe couldn't give us a tunnel—just a deep trench scored into the hill. But it worked very well. We covered the roof with branches and bracken, sealed it with earth, and had our sett. Burt chugged off down the valley for fishcakes and *Sesame Street* and left us to it. We wriggled inside, and tried to be a bit more authentic.

Although many setts are echoing labyrinths, coiling like a bundle of earthworms deep around rocks and roots, some are not. The simplest sort, dug as temporary shelters, are single tunnels. Like the medieval gates that turn through right angles to prevent a rush of invaders from getting any momentum, they turn, a yard or so from the entrance, push on for a bit, and then bell out at the far end, where there's a sleeping chamber. That's what ours was like. We shaped it with our paws and with a child's beach spade (ideal for working in small spaces). We tried to scuffle out the earth with our hind legs, but we couldn't, because the ceiling was authentically low (most setts are roughly semicircular in profile, being wider than they're high). Tom could pull the bracken bedding in backward, as proper badgers always do, but it was too much for me. And we sneezed: constantly, mightily, and unbadgerishly. Badgers seem to have some sort of muscular sphincter just before the entrance to the nostrils that they can close up when they're digging to keep the earth from getting in. But we haven't, and in that dry July, at least at the top of the tunnel, it was terrible. When they're hunting snufflingly through the world, nose to the ground, badgers of course can't use that merciful sphincter: they need the scent to reach their nostrils. And then they blast out the dust in heavy snorts. That, between sneezes, is what we did as we excavated. Tom was filling tissues with silica and blood for a week.

We used headlamps. Badgers have more photoreceptive rods in their retinas than we do, and they have a reflective layer in their eyes, called a tapetum, that makes their eyes shine in car headlights and that bounces uncollected photons back into the retina. Badgers squeeze more light from their world into their brains than we do. The world gives them the same; they do more with it. The near dark of our midday tunnel would have been dazzling to them.

It was hard work, but eventually we were done. We crawled down to the river, lapped from a pool where leeches waved at our lips, and crawled back to our chamber, where we fell asleep, side by side and head to toe, as all good badgers do. It makes the best use of the space. Tom always moved in the night. "Feet in the face aren't friendly," he said.

I dreamed: the florid, in-your-face dreams that lie just beneath consciousness. The sort of dreams you get in the tropics, when things in green and gold dance to the beat of the ceiling fan. Here, though, the beat was Tom's heart against my head, and the tune was the low hum of the hill and the girl's voice of the river.

I don't doubt for a moment that badgers have some sort of consciousness. One of the reasons is that I've seen them sleeping. There's plainly something going on in their heads when they're asleep. They paddle, yip, and snarl; the full repertoire of expressions plays out on their faces. There is some sort of story being enacted. And what can the central character be but the badger's *self*? The misty land of sleep is where our own selves, so often suppressed, denied, and violated, walk proud and have an uninterrupted voice.

It's no doubt true that the dreaming badger is processing data from the day or night just gone, trying out, for evolutionarily obvious reasons, the way in which it might, in the light of the new data, respond to future challenges. But this dry formulation doesn't elbow out the self: far from it. The self is the substrate of the concerns that are being addressed.

I've often thought that sleep must be doing something like a defragmentation program on a computer. Files are being shifted from where the day has dumped them to the cabinets from which they can be more easily extracted. When I self-hypnotize, my eyelids flicker in hypnotism's emulation of Rapid Eye Movement sleep, and the flickering is just like the flickering of the little red light when the defrag program is running. Indeed, I can feel the defrag. But the analogy is not complete. A defrag program doesn't need a story. Sleeping badgers have stories, and stories need subjects.

What might it mean for an unconscious creature to dream? Indeed to sleep at all? What's being lost when "consciousness" is lost? What accompanies the creature into the world beyond the veil? If badgers aren't conscious in a sense comparable to us, their sleeping smiles and winces are more inscrutable than consciousness itself. I prefer the lesser mystery.

* * *

We awoke in stages (or became more evenly awake, since the wild won't usually abandon you utterly to unconsciousness: there's too much happening), to the rattling of a jay and, more fully, to the growling of an engine. It was Burt, with fish pie.

"Bogus, I know, but I won't tell anyone."

In fact it wasn't bogus at all. Badgers are the ultimate opportunistic omnivores. No badger would turn up its nose at fish pie.

"I'll tell you what, though," he went on. "To compensate, I'll come down later and set the dogs on you. And then we'll go up to the road and I'll try to run you over."

Yes, very amusing. Yet the point was serious. I'd tended to think that a badger's life was painted in the colors of the wood. These colors I could hope to see, too. But there was a darker color there—the color of fear. You see that color—a pale electric blue in my mind's eye—on the edges of bristling fur when a badger stops on its path through the fern, having got a nose full of human stench, and around the tips of straining ears as it hears a dog that's slightly nearer than the usual farm dog.

By killing all the wolves, we have appointed ourselves as

the badger's prime tormentor. If badgers do dream, we appear in their worst nightmares—unless they revert in sleep to the distant times when wolves hunted badgers down to a final snarling stand against the bole of an oak. Memories live a long time in wild heads. Red deer panic wildly if you let them sniff lion dung, although it's been millennia since lions were a worry.

In fact I doubt that badgers dream of wolves. Badgers have altered their lives significantly to take account of their wolflessness, and I'd expect their psyches to follow their behavior. Where there are wolves (in the more howling parts of eastern Europe, for instance), badgers aren't the bustlingly communal animals they are here. There aren't the big ancestral palaces in well-drained hillsides. Instead, badgers live in smaller, more intimate, less playful units. If there are wolves out there, badgers tend to take nervous, prudent, straight-line journeys, which reduces the amount of foraging and so reduces the number of badgers an area can hold. True, big setts are convenient for psychopaths with pit bulls, but psychopaths are less efficient predators than wolves, and they don't like to stray too far from roads. Wales can be vile to badgers, but it's a happier place than Belarus.

If something as fundamental as community structure can change with a change of prime predator, I'd have thought that dreams would change, too. The dream life of a badger must reflect the emotional color of the wood, and a wood with wolves is all red and black.

Professional biologists don't like talking about animal *emotion*. Mention the word, and there's a collective indrawing of breath over those mellifluous academic tongues, a stadium wave of raised eyebrows, and an exchange of pitying glances as they acknowledge that the benighted speaker isn't one of the club. It's fine to talk about animal cognition, because that sort of talk is comfortably grounded in the sole and tyrannous metaphor used by mainstream behaviorists—and *by* which they are used: the computer. Chat about an animal as a piece of hardware running (or even being) a bit of software, and you'll meet only smiles. It's fine to talk about indices of welfare: about the rising of corticosteroid levels in unhappy (sorry, stressed) cows. But emotion: no.

There was one biologist who didn't share this distaste. He was a fine naturalist, a sympathetic and unsentimental observer who wasn't marinated in Darwinist reductionism at the university. His name was Charles Darwin, and he wrote a splendid and almost unread book called *The Expression of Emotions in Animals.* Here he is, in a gently swashbuckling mood:

> Sir C. Bell evidently wished to draw as broad a distinction as possible between man and the lower animals; and he consequently asserts that with "the lower creatures there is no expression but what may be referred, more or less plainly, to their acts of volition or necessary instincts." He further maintains that their faces "seem chiefly capable of expressing rage and fear." But man himself cannot express love and humility by external signs so plainly as does a dog, when with drooping ears, hanging lips, flexuous body, and wagging tail, he meets his beloved master. Nor can these movements in the dog be explained by acts of volition or necessary instincts, any more than the beaming eyes and smiling cheeks of a man when he meets an old friend. If Sir C. Bell had been questioned about the expression of affection in the dog, he would no doubt have answered that this animal had been created with special instincts, adapting him for association with man, and that all further enquiry on the subject was superfluous.

That's near the beginning of Darwin's quite long book. He thought further inquiry about true emotion in animals far from superfluous. That's what happens when you do your biology in the real, growling, aching, joyous world, rather than being locked up in a paradigm.

When I experience a pleasurable stimulus, my facial muscles contract in a particular way. When a dog experiences a stimulus that indicates a benefit to the dog that is comparable to the benefit of which my pleasure is an index, its facial muscles contract in a more or less identical way. Just listen to how careful I'm being to speak the language of the academy. Isn't it absurd? Shouldn't we whip out Occam's razor, and the editorial blue pencil, and talk about animal pleasure?

And if pleasure, why not other emotions, too?

Anyone who has ever watched dogs playing or cats smooching or swifts doing thermodynamically fatuous things just for the screaming, exulting, rapturous hell of it will have read this discussion with baffled disbelief. They won't need my cautious reasoning to conclude that when animal faces do something identical to ours in response to a stimulus that we can recognize as noxious, there's probably something going on at an "emotional" level that is comparable to what we'd experience. It would be odd beyond belief if natural selection had conferred on us alone the emotional corollaries of the ways our worlds are.

But this is not a mandate for anthropomorphism. To say that something is comparable is not to say that it's the same. That is perhaps particularly the case for fear. The color of my fear is not recognizably the same as even the color of the fear of other humans.

Although the color of badger fear is that shrill, strident, unforgettable blue, it is not the predominant color of their world. It may be a penumbra around the edges of their tumbling, their lust, and their hunger, as the spiky gray knowledge of my own eventual annihilation is around mine.

Do they, too, fear personal extinction? They certainly don't want to die, as the mangled face of many a terrier will tell.

But what is it that doesn't want to stop? Is there an elaborate magical dialogue between the badger and its genes, along the lines of "You're our bearer: if you're taken out, it's all up for us. So put up a good show, won't you, for our sakes?" "Oh, all right then: you're the boss"? That's the sort of conversation that much of biology tends tacitly to assume.

I prefer a simpler and less fashionable version, which admits that a badger has a real sense of self, and real pleasures that it judges as outweighing its pains. Badgers are philosophers. They have an idea of the Good Life, which presumes there is a self that can lead that life. This is a self that doesn't want to lose the neurological joys of nuzzling cubs, or the smell of wild garlic, or the smack of earthworms against the tongue. Insist if you like that all these things are the payment given by the genes for the mercenary services in their defense of the strong-jawed phenotype. That's fine. Your insistence doesn't dispose of the self, or the Goodness of the Life that self leads.

* * *

We put the fish pie in a plastic box and put it in the river to keep cool. The box wasn't terribly badgerish, but then again badgers, although they're enthusiastic scavengers, seem to prefer their carrion fresh—even though carcasses that are further gone have the added garnish of maggots, which you'd have thought badgers would think of as children think of chocolate drops sprinkled on pudding. I doubt it's the risk of infection that inhibits them. Badgers lose their immunological naïveté very quickly and don't spend their lives throwing up into the ferns. All thoughtful human parents should mix pureed earthworms with the milk: it'd abolish asthma and eczema, and exorcise later fears of a bad curry. But badgers, like many animals and some people, can vomit, when necessary, without much distress: they hardly break stride. I'd like to be like that.

Having stowed the pie, we stumbled up the bank and hollowed out a nest in the bracken. The stems soared above us like the fluted columns of a devastated cathedral. Green light slid algally over Tom's face and neck, decomposing him. Less poetically, a sheep tick scuttled under his shirt. Ticks are always in a hurry. I pulled up the shirt and watched, interested to see what site it would choose. They tend to go for my groin or my armpit, which seems logical, but our children tend to get them somewhere obvious on their torsos, which doesn't seem to be. Though perhaps the poorer innervation there means that they're less likely to be detected, and there's no abrasion from a moving joint or a swinging scrotum. Sure enough, this one, though it could have had the discreet dampness of an armpit, began to get settled over a rib. I crushed it between my nails.

Having Tom next to me made me pretty immune to ticks. They go for him every time. It's presumably a scent thing: they head for him rather than me long before they can know that his skin is thinner and that they won't have to fight through a noxious jungle of oily hair.

Many badgers carry ticks—typically hedgehog, dog, and sheep ticks—although the incidence isn't as high as one might think. The leathery skin must be a challenge, and ticks tend to concentrate around the thin skin of the anus and perineum rather than, as in dogs, on the head, the neck, and the thin skin of the underbelly and the inner thighs.

Lying up outside the sett during the day isn't unbadgerish, although it's far from the rule. Badgers sometimes, just like we did, crawl into dense vegetation and lie there until dusk comes and it's time for the next round of shuffle-hunting. We don't know why that is. Perhaps there's tension at home, and they can't bear the thought of a day close to wretched, cantankerous, odious X. And sometimes, no doubt, they've been caught short a long way from home as dawn breaks and don't want to run the gauntlet of the early morning dog walkers.

Cubs in particular play outside during the day. It's their version of teenage rebellion, like adolescent humans staying out inconsiderately late at night. I don't imagine, though, that those days in the open are very relaxing ones. Although dangers hover around the sett, they are dangers faced in community, using old and practiced strategies. Aloneness, novelty, and sunlight are the badger's unholy trinity. Badgers are social to the core, and conservative, and creatures of shadow. Sunlight freezes them. It seems to switch off their senses. You can often walk right up to a daytime badger. It'll seem stunned. They are two-mode animals: on and off. They live in the no-man's-land between day and night, and that's such a demanding place there's no room for halfheartedness.

Tom needed to sleep, and so he did, curled fetally on old bracken, his paws, earth-brown from digging, clasped under his chin. I, too, needed to sleep, and so I didn't. Instead, like one of those sun-stunned day badgers, I watched nothing in particular; I was a lump of idling software in a box made of meat.

We often did this when we were in the wood. We had to change our rhythm to that of the badgers, which meant sleeping in the day, but, at least at first, I found the sett a threatening place. Was this a primordial fear of burial? If so, it was a strange fear. Live burial has never been a common method of execution, and my human ancestors lived in and took refuge in caves for millennia. Burial's associated with death, and most of us are afraid not of death but of dying. The idea of physical dissolution is more interesting than terrifying. Although we're conservative animals, for whom the novel thought of being eaten and assimilated demands a bit of psychological adjustment, it's not the stuff of lasting, soul-shaping horror. It was more likely to be a fear of losing that long view that our long legs give us—the view that makes us creatures of the big horizon, and hence of infinite options. To be is to see is to stride is to be able to choose. Even the panic of claustrophobia, which I've known when squeezing through a tight rock tunnel somewhere under Derbyshire, is really an unhappiness that one's options are limited.

The walls of our sett writhed around me, as active as a uterus, but not so comforting. The earth twisted and fumbled and scrabbled and sprouted and spurted. A worm fell into my mouth. A badger would have welcomed it as a pasha on his couch welcomes a grape dropped by a slave, even though the worm is probably made of the badger's dead grandmother entombed in the sett wall. I gagged quietly and went back to sleep with my face buried in the bracken bedding.

Those first few days and nights underground taught me a lot. They taught me that, despite my shaggy, anarchic pretensions, I was dismally suburban: I preferred a whitewashed wall to the endless change and fascination of a real earth wall, and regimented ranks of floral wallpaper patterns to the Real Thing. In fact, and this was the main worry, I preferred almost any confection to the Real Thing. I preferred my ideas of badgers and the wild to real badgers and real wilderness. They demanded much less. They were more obedient and less complex. And they didn't broadcast my inadequacies so deafeningly.

These were all symptoms of a nasty condition, from which I'd thought I was immune: colonialism. "You shall have dominion over the fish of the sea, and the birds of the air, and over the cattle, and over all the earth, and over every creeping thing that creeps upon the earth," we're assured. Taken on its own, as it has been, this is a catastrophic formulation. You can go straight from Genesis 1 to the Monsanto boardroom, pausing for sightseeing picnics at the annihilation of the world's herd game, at some select dust bowls full of cucumbers grown in nitrate powder, at the *Torrey Canyon* wreck, at factory farms, at the edge of a retreating glacier, and at many other uplifting destinations. And you could take in, while on the road, the sport hunting of native peoples everywhere, since they're not made in the image of God, are they?

I'd sanctimoniously seen myself as a bandanna-clad fighter against this sort of perverted biblicism. And yet here I was, lying resentfully in my burrow, thinking exactly the thoughts that I theoretically despised. I'd thought that I was better than the wild, more advanced, an improvement on it, evolution's zenith.

I learned some other things, too. One was that all humans, at some level, know the absurdity of the human pretension, know that there's a better way than colonialism. Here's the proof. Take a sleek, besuited banker, ideally fresh from Stuttgart or Zurich. Put him in a wood. Drop into his polished palm, with an explanation, a nice dry otter spraint or a handful of fox droppings. He'll examine them and sniff them respectfully. Now do the same with a domestic dog turd. He'll throw down the turd and throw up his expensive lunch. This shows that he's not irredeemably far from acknowledging the generic nobility of savagery, or hopelessly out of touch with his indwelling noble savage. The dog shit draws out his inchoate distaste for the domestic.

I learned, too, that real, lasting change is possible—to our appetites, our fears, and our views. And that change has to happen in that order. First I learned to like that burrow. Habit is tremendously powerful. It can do almost anything. Merely going regularly into the sett and having a place at the end pressed to the shape of my body was enough to change my appetite for underground living. From that low platform I could jump to more complex forms of appreciation: liking the shape of the window on the sunlit world that was the tunnel's end; liking the exuberant spectrum of smells that met my nose as I crawled from a dusty bracken bed, through a stretch of hay, up through a cervix of earth and leaf mold and out, panting from the effort of the crawl, into elder and oak and, very often (since Tom's a pyromaniac), wood smoke. And then, since it is hard to fear what one likes, all that swirling atavistic panic slowly cleared. I didn't hyperventilate if I wasn't on my actual and metaphorical hind legs, manfully scanning distant vistas and making sense of and plans for the big picture. It was okay to lie in the dark, surrounded by the scratching and humming and thrashing of animals that would one day eat me. From there it was a small enough step not to mind being eaten, and not to mind being in, or getting toward, the state in which one is eaten. And once you're there, you're at last a proper ecologist, knowing your place, all ecocolonialism gone. Only then, at the end of a weary and distressing metaphysical road, can you really begin the business of being a badger.

Quite a lot of being a badger consisted simply in allowing the wood to do to us what it did to a badger; being there when it rained; keeping badgers' hours; being cramped underground (there's no possibility of thinking that the world is at your sovereign feet when in fact it's over your head, squashing your legs, and dropping into your eyes); letting the bluebells brush your face instead of your boots. But there were some high physiological fences keeping us out of the badger's world. The main one was scent.

My landscape is a visual one. I have big eyes and a correspondingly big visual processing area in my brain. The version of the world that my brain constructs has a high proportion of visual elements. These are supplemented importantly by the results of my cognitive processing—so that when I say I see a hill, it's a very different hill from that which anyone else would describe. I "see" the hill through a set of "higher" cortical filters: myths, presumptions, recollections, cross-references, allusions. There are ways of stripping out those filters. Many of the ways come from the East, and I've used some of them over the years. It's possible, though hard, to learn to see a flower. But when you do, it's still *seeing*.

A badger's landscape is primarily a scent landscape. The main bricks that its brain uses to build its world are made in its nose. The physical boundaries of its life are set by scent. Its territories are marked by defecation, and the feces of each badger carry a unique scent. We're all, all the time, bacterial substrates, and bacteria do slightly, or dramatically (everyone's been in a hot train compartment with an unwashed, undeodorized teenager), different things with each of us. It's the same with badgers. Each has its own olfactory hallmark—a cocktail of the musky caudal gland secretion and the work of bacteria.

But it's not only perimeters that matter. Noses don't just map perimeters: they sneeze form, color, and personality into the badger's life. For a badger, with its relatively poor eyesight, wood sorrel is mainly the scent of wood sorrel; a soaring hornbeam has, on a hot day, the helical shape of the scent vortex that pulls dust up into the canopy, and is, on a cool day, a low hump of tart lichen with an indistinct chimney. A dead hedgehog is the shape of hedgehog, then the shape of green scent, then the shape of tripe, then the shape of sweet, then the shape of pork scratchings, then the shape of beetle.

The literary way into this should be the autobiographical reflections of synesthetes—those who smell colors, or taste numbers, or whose letters each have a color of their own. But that literature (and I don't exclude Nabokov, who wrote exhaustingly about synesthesia) is strangely unpoetic and unreflective. It's as if the gift of perceiving the world in several dimensions disables the ability to describe it. Or perhaps their world is beyond words, which doesn't bode well for this book, or for any other attempt to grope at extreme otherness. The most audacious and hence the least unsuccessful artistic effort was by Olivier Messiaen, who devised a new musical mode to demonstrate what it's like to live in two overlapping sensory zones.

Compared to a badger, humans are almost entirely olfactorily blind. We perceive scent landscapes in terms not even of outlines, but of vague assemblies of blocks with wholly indistinct margins. Imagine walking down a city street and seeing, instead of faces and figures, a swaying tartan rug. That's what our scent perception is like.

But I didn't quite despair. I remembered that humans are very plastic creatures, and that blind people can learn to echolocate. Not well enough to make a chapter on bats credible, but well enough to avoid banging into walls. That's what the *tap, tap, tap* of the white stick does: it bounces off obstacles and back to the brain, which crudely assembles the information into a picture of the world ahead. And I remembered Jack Schwartz, who said that he could see auras around each of us, and whose ability to detect light frequencies extended from 335 to 1,700 nanometers, which is a thousand nanometers beyond the spectrum normally regarded as visible by humans. But I remembered in particular John Adams, the physiologist who tested Schwartz. Astonished at the results, he reexamined his own vision without the conventional presumptions about what humans could do, and found that much of the theoretically invisible infrared spectrum was in fact visible to him.

I tried strenuously to turn myself into a more olfactory creature. I joined a blind-tasting wine society, and aahed and imaginatively adjectivized with the rest. I burned a different brand of incense in each room of the house, trying to supplement my visual picture of each room with an olfactory one, and trying to learn how the air currents in the house crept and surged. I held blind smellings of my children's clothes. I put a different type of cheese in each corner of a room, moved all the furniture so that there were no other clues, blindfolded and disoriented myself, and then tried to find out where I was by reference only to the cheese. When engaged in middle-class cheek kissing, I tried to get a good sniff. I snipped off different types of leaves each day and put them on the pillow at night. But most of all I lay outside with my nose on and at various levels above the ground, learning how scent changes through the day and through the seasons and over the immense distance between the ground and the normal elevation of my nose.

Water unlocks scent. Sprinkle water on Saharan sand and you'll be right back in a primordial sea. After a rainstorm in limestone country you get nosefuls of long-dead shrimp. And it's water that makes the rest of the world breathe, too—a botanical truism, yes, but also a sensory fact. By the early morning the summer ground is relatively cold, and the water that condenses on it makes the ground truly smell of itself. Dry ground is just waiting to be realized. As the day heats up the ground rises, sometimes very fast, until you've got the huntsman's celebrated "breast-high scent"—the scent that gets hounds charging, often too drunk with the scent to speak. This pure scent doesn't rise much farther than a hound's shoulder or a badger's head. By the time the sun has lifted the land that high, it's also made the air eddy and tumble and slide around, so that everything higher than a couple of feet above the ground isn't so local. By seven o'clock in June a badger, caught out after a hard night's worming, will have the treetops and the pondweed from across the valley.

It's different in winter. Then there's not that exhilarating gradient down which the earth can slip up into the air. Scent takes refuge in the soil, like everything else that can burrow. And even there scent is sluggish. When we hacked our way back to the sett through the mid-December tinsel, the chill choked the scent. Or perhaps it just anesthetized our noses. Neurons don't work so well at low temperatures. The manufacturers of lager that tastes of nothing insist, very wisely, that it should be drunk ice cold: it's the only way they'll not be found out.

When the temperature fell in the evening, the ground, which had been soaking up calories all day, retained its heat for longer than the air, and indeed the cold air above the ground seemed to act as a blanket, pressing scent tightly to the earth. That's very good for badgers, who are mainly interested in things on and slightly below the ground. And it's one of the main reasons why badgers come out when the sun goes down.

My attempt to enter the scent world was partially successful. But there were obvious and frustrating limits. I could, and did, learn to pay more attention to scent, and I knew glimmeringly, for full, fat fragments of a moment, what a landscape painted in scent might look like. But these glimmerings were imaginative extrapolations from what I actually sensed. The limiting factor was the magnitude of the inputs. I couldn't multiply the number or the sensitivity of my sense receptors to anything approximating those of a badger. All I could do was to say: "Well, if inputs totaling x do that, what would inputs totaling one thousand x do?"

Relating all this is hard. It would be pointless to reel off the adjectives and metaphors I used to describe to myself the scent of shepherd's purse on the pillow, or dog's mercury in the wood. That might say something about me, but nothing about badgers or woods.

Do badgers use adjectives? I expect that they describe the world to themselves, and so they must. Their world isn't just a huge damp noun, a big blob of "is-ness." Adjectives are a corollary of fine shades of perception.

Metaphors are a different matter. They demand a lot of central processing power. Badgers have a fair amount, but they've got other, and probably better, things to do with theirs than the industry of metaphor—the forging of connections between disparate things in the world, and the use of those connections. Metaphors are useful for big-leap strategy and hence for coping with traumatic novelty. But normally badgers are creatures of routine: sleep, wake, stretch, defecate in one of the sett's prescribed lavatories or on the boundaries of the territory, eat earthworms, sleep, repeat. It wouldn't add anything to this process to say, en route, that a tree was a mother.

All of which is to say that the ways in which, inevitably, I perceive and describe a badger's scent world involve things that have no representative at all in the badger's own world. They are purely human artifice. This is the main source of inauthenticity.

But perhaps it's not really so bad. For, like most organisms, a badger isn't particularly interested in dog's mercury, per se. The smell of dog's mercury is immediately and dramatically translated into something very different—to something like "When I got to this point last night, about twenty steps farther on, and a bit to the right, was an old log, and underneath that there were some fat earthworms. I had some, but there may well be more." I can't know what the immediate burst of dog's mercury scent does in a badger's brain, but does it really matter? I can arrive at a pretty decent approximation to what it *means*. I can't do much to educate my senses (although I can do something to educate what my brain does with its inputs), but I can get better at translating external stimuli into the basic propositions of badgerese.

* * *

A few days after dumping us, Burt roared back with chorizo and news. The news was about some figures on some national balance sheet, and about an imminent storm. I couldn't have cared less about the figures, which was progress. But I did care about the storm. "And remember," said Burt, as he climbed back into the Land Rover and made off, "you've got to be naked: butt naked."

In chapter 1 I sang the praises of nakedness, and of Fraser Darling's bare feet. I don't take back a word, but Burt was wrong. Badgers have a thick outer coat of coarse hair lying over a softer inner layer. Both trap air very efficiently. The badger walks around in a halo of warm air. To strip off would take me a long way from the badger's sensory world. I was much closer to it in my old moleskins and tweed coat. In which, as soon as Burt had gone, I went to sleep, deep at the far end of the sett.

We'd not been in the wood long, but already it was ours. It was that sense of proprietorship, rather than any concern about physical dangers, that made us emerge cautiously from the sett at dusk, sniffing the air exactly as badgers do. Outraged proprietorship feels like danger.

Our beds were now in the ground. We came out of the ground every day, and we wanted to stay close to it all the time. I'd thought that it would seem an absurd pretension to go on hands and knees through the wood. Now it would have seemed an insufferable arrogance to do otherwise. And not just that: we had begun to know how much we'd be missing. To go hind-legged would have been like watching the wood on TV when we'd been offered the best seats in the stalls.

Our heads swayed from side to side as we came out of the sett—exactly the questing swing of a badger, but forced by our clumsy anatomy. Those long legs and arms felt as disabling as amputations. We were going through bracken, reeds, and rough grass. I'd dropped six feet and several million years into the badger's world. My versions of the senses that were most useful down here—scent and hearing—were dismal compared to a badger's. I was handling the badger's world with thick mittens. But even so, this world was objectively more interesting than my own. A lot more happens at six inches and below than at six feet and above.

It was obvious why natural selection had made the choices it had. Eyes were pretty pointless down here. I couldn't see more than a few inches ahead. The space inside the cranium is prime real estate. It would have been foolish to hand more of it over to visual processing. My eyes, even in the fast-fading light, were better than a badger's. When I raised my head I could see bats flickering in and out of the lacework of the oaks, and a barn owl ghosting over the walls in the field across the river, and wood pigeons settling fussily in for the night. These had no place in the badger's night. Badgers trade these airy pleasures for darker, stickier, mucusy, damper, rougher pleasures. Dropping my head was like going from Schubert in the conservatoire to a candlelit bordello where you wade through beer to the bed. If I had to pick one word for the badger's experience, it would be *intimate*. Grass and bracken stems brush your face. When you're forcing a new path, every step is like a birth. Water shudders off grass into your eyes. Things slide away. Slide, hop, rush. You don't just absorb the world; you make it. You make the fear that rustles away on every side.

When a badger goes out, its object is to bump into food. This system of incontinent collision with the wood makes the badger more a creature of the wood than any other inhabitant. We bustled and grunted and elbowed and pushed and pressed our noses into the ground. And even *we* smelled something: the citrusy piss of the voles in their runs within the grass; the distantly maritime tang of a slug trail, like a winter rock pool; the crushed laurel of a frog; the dustiness of a toad; the sharp musk of a weasel; the blunter musk of an otter; and the fox, whose smell is red to the least synesthetic man alive. But most of all we had what we clumsily called the earth: leaves and dung and corpses and houses and rain and eggs and horrors.

We got these things usually as single words, occasionally as short sentences. If we had noses like badgers' they would have been intricate stories, weaving in and out of one another, punctuated by possibility and frustration.

When Tom and I snuffled through the wood on our first few nights, I began to feel trapped by my visualness. As I got occasional nose-glimpses of the wood, and became able to guess at some of what I was missing, this became the full-blown panic, regret, and bereavement of the prisoner. I made ludicrous, mystical plans for escape. They failed. The sensory claustrophobia has never abated. When, now, I pray for redemption, a redeemed nose is high up on the list of petitions.

Making something of the badger's auditory world wasn't quite so hopeless. Badgers have much better sensitivity to high frequencies than we do. They probably hear sounds up to around 60,000 Hz, whereas even the most acute human children won't go much beyond around 25,000 Hz, and many humans of sixty plus will stop at about 8,000 Hz. Badgers will pick up many of the squeaks of a bank vole, inaudible to us. But a squeak isn't unimaginable. I live in a house full of them. And squeaks aren't all that badgers hear. We share most, but not all, of the badger's bandwidth. The badger notes the pheasants exploding from the edge of the field; the thump of the generator up at the house; the mewing of the wood warblers; the panic of a sheep caught in the wire; and the grumble of distant thunder. At least, their ears register these things, and there is electrical activity in the auditory parts of their brain cortices shortly afterward. What does the individual badger "hear" as a result of the changing pressures on its tympanum that we choose to call a sound? Strictly speaking, I have no idea. I have no idea what Mozart sounds like to anyone apart from me (and even that sound changes massively with my state of digestion). This isn't a problem of physiology; it's the problem of otherness, which we inadequately physiologize as a difficulty in inquiring into the nature of complex central processing. We can't know that we're not alone. It is an act of pure faith for me to declare that there are some things I share with my children and my best friends. And I choose similarly to believe that a badger *hears* those pheasants instead of merely noting them. In the case of my children and friends my choice is supported to some degree by EEGs and auditory stem potentials and functional MRI scans (although there are no such data, so far as I know, for badgers). But the support is very limited, and I can't blame anyone for not joining me in my act of faith.

We're probably safe in saying, though, that the badgers weren't very interested in the generator. They habituate very quickly to sounds, especially distant ones, that they know aren't threatening. The thump inevitably caused the eardrum to vibrate: that's immutable physics. But the brain ignored it; that's excitingly mutable biology. The brain chose not to use that block in building its world. The plaintive wood warblers had a place but not, normally, at the level of "conscious" hearing. Theirs was the mew of a normal wood. A change in their tone might indicate something relevant, and hence it was change, rather than the wood warbler per se, to which the badger paid attention. I, not knowing the significance of the changed tone, and lacking context generally, paid attention to more than the badger did. In this sense my wood was bigger and more complex than the badger's. A badger focuses fairly hard on its career of survival, and focus is rarely a friend of aesthetics. A badger's aesthetics, I would guess, are mainly relational and fairly crudely sensual. They like rolling around with the kids and scratching their bellies in the sun.

That's not to say that they can't branch out. If I can expand my suite of sensory accomplishments and appreciations, why shouldn't a badger? Music is the obvious thought. Pan piped more than he spoke. If Bach encodes (and surely he does) some of the most basic formulae of this dazzling world, wouldn't you expect him to do exciting things in a Welsh wood? If he makes my DNA quiver, shouldn't he set the DNA of a badger—so, so similar to mine—a-trembling?

I've tried this, halfheartedly and inconclusively. My speakers have always been rained on, or the batteries too flat for a proper broadcast. But most classical-music-loving dog owners are on my side. That cliché Jack Russell listening to His Master's Voice would learn to love the B Minor Mass just as much as the voice, even if the Mass didn't normally come with a pat and a handful of dog biscuits. In the film *The Weeping Camel*, the mother camel, which had refused to allow its calf to suckle, is entranced by an old Mongolian song and becomes immediately happy and compliant. The calf suckles and lives. The mother permits suckling, and so lives as a mother. The music represents the way that things should be, and the world, including the camel, hums along. The music acts like a defibrillator, gently shocking the world back into rhythm. Great music, great literature, great anything, are great because they are built of the most basic elements; because they are fundamental. They can therefore speak to kings and commoners, badgers and wood warblers. Hence this next and most extravagant act of faith: play the B Minor Mass to a badger, and the badger would hear the B Minor Mass.

Badgers don't just have broader bandwidth than we do; their sensitivity to sounds within the audible bandwidth is also greater. They're more acute. It's thought that they may be able to hear, as many birds do, the rasp of the earthworms' bristles as they scratch through the earth.

Just think what the obscene tsunami of a nearby motor vehicle does to an animal that can do that. It's easy to get a faint idea. Sit outdoors one night in an isolated place. Leave the iPod at home for once. Then walk quietly to a road. The first car will seem like a regiment of tanks. You'll feel violated, and feel that the land is violated. You'll note in yourself, perhaps with surprise, that since both you and the land are violated, there must be a previously unrecognized solidarity between you and the land. Or even, since nights outside tend to make you romantic, perhaps you'll think that you and the land share an *identity*. You'll hate and resent the driver. But, most of all, you'll pity him, cocooned in his air-conditioning, listening to canned banality on the radio. You'll know, and have, what he's lost. And you'll know something of the outrage of the badger feeling the bellow of the engine in its ears, the trembling of the road in its feet, and the whole bloody bombardment in all of it, deep down and throughout—rape, offense, invasion. Badgers feel low-frequency sounds in their feet. A distant footfall in a darkening wood shudders into their pads. They freeze, which isn't a great strategy in front of a bus, until reassured (easily done in the wood by scratching: they love the sounds of normality). In the road there's no reassurance for any of us.

* * *

A big black bale, full of the worst that Nova Scotia could find, bundled toward us. It shuddered over Snowdon, spilling some salty Atlantic shavings, and then spun on, up and up until the sharp green air over the wood slashed through its electric sheet. Down it rolled, angry and old, bundling up rain, dust, feathers, and swaths of insects like a big baler and sealing them all in an electric sheet instead of a piece of plastic. Tom and I, noses to ground, felt its approach in the back of our necks. The sun fell through a tense and sickly sky.

There was a businesslike urgency in the wood—a hurry to feed off the usual before the unusual arrived. It was a good crammer for the olfactorially remedial student. As the light went we found ourselves in intimate tunnels of touch and scent. The world outside the tunnel was made of sound, but as we crawled and sniffed it seemed increasingly distant and irrelevant, and when the rain came, the shocking reports on the leaves all around our heads were a fusillade that dismissed all of that bigger context. There was no way of hearing the scrambling of the wood pigeons in the next-door field. There were just our heads, and around them a halo, with a radius of about six inches, of hiss, crack, mumble, and scent. The fusillade split open the ground. Scent came spinning out so fast that it reached even our noses. It was as if the ground were bursting to tell the story of that summer. A badger's nose can detect the tales of each of the actors in the drama of the wood; we got a muddled medley, new and thrilling to us. Yes, I know that there is no such thing as a play without players; that if you cut away the particular you're left not with the generic but with nothing; that the generic is a monstrous abstraction from which I'd come to the wood to escape. Yet I couldn't help thinking that what was rising into my nose *was* the summer, or that that conclusion was better than no conclusion at all.

The *rat-a-tat* of the rain had summoned the earthworms as a military parade drummer draws the crowds. The earth opened up and out they oozed, dripping from the hill like mucus candles from a snotty-nosed child.

These rain-time worm bonanzas must create an agonizing dilemma in the badger's mind. The wood becomes a groaning smorgasbord, but you have to get wet to feast. Badgers are cozy creatures. Their default setting is curled up with the others, dry and asleep in a bed of old bracken, deep inside a well-drained hillside. That setting can be overridden, but it takes a lot of doing. The worms were safe that night. We followed the badgers into our piece of hill.

* * *

I lay at the mouth of the sett. It had a curtain of water, like those curtains of bead strands that fill the doors leading to the toilets in small Chinese restaurants. It was almost completely dark—at least to my collection of rods—except when lightning bled through the fault lines in the sky. Yet each water droplet seemed to act like a retina, sucking light efficiently from the wood and reflecting it onto my own grateful retinas, buried in my head, buried in the hill.

Our sett was cradled in the interlocking fingers of tree roots: beech on either side, oak from above. The whole wood bent to the wind. There was no overground or underground: it was all just ground. We rocked in our cradle, the roots around us straining and creaking like the timbers of a rolling ship. A wood mouse, displaced from a flooded or crumbling tunnel, scrambled in and hunched, shivering, in the crook of Tom's knee.

Without that wood mouse I wouldn't have slept. But it reassured me. We were in the best place—a sanctuary accredited by the wild—and so I snatched bits of queasy maritime sleep, which, laid end to end, were enough. Tom slept, which is what I expect badgers do in storms.

The storm didn't devastate: it culled. Some branches that had brazenly reached too high were wrenched hubristically down. Some trees that had imprudently spent their sun sugar on leaves rather than roots were weighed in the wind's balance and found wanting. The river snarled brown, and a dead crow circled the pool, as if looking for carrion on the gravel. But Nova Scotia's worst wasn't so bad.

Our sett wasn't damaged at all, but out of gratitude to it, and with a new proprietorial pride in having survived the worst of the summer, we set to that morning to make it even better. We excavated a new chamber, complete with shelves, reinforced the roof, and built an imposing earth arch at the entrance. Then, as Tom was happily making his own purely recreational earthworks, I slipped into unbroken sleep.

I'd thought that this pattern (sleeping in the day, being

out and about at night) would be hard to establish. I knew, of course, that I could slowly reset my own clock. That was a simple enough matter of cortisol levels. But I'd thought that the change would be psychologically strenuous—that I'd resent the loss of the sun so much that simply to exist as a nocturnal animal would be an act of exhausting protest against all my instincts.

It wasn't so. The cortisol took about four days to fall fully into line, but after a mere two I was willing it to obedience. There was nothing very profound about this: it was the simple lust of the curious tourist. That first night of nosiness, frustrating though it was, had shown me (no, that's a visual word; had "indicated"? Too generic. We need an olfactory version of "shown," and there isn't one)—had *demonstrated* (weak, but the best I can do) that within that wood there was a vertiginously strange and achingly desirable universe, untrodden and untreadable by man in his normal sensorineural boots. I wanted it badly.

This wasn't part of the poignant true-love quest for otherness, which wants to know in the desperate hope of being known. It was an Elizabethan desire to discover a new world. When I slid out of the sett each night I was setting sail from Plymouth Hoe and heading west into the sunset in the hope of fame, spices, and, importantly, somewhere new to live.

* * *

Burt trundled back, not looking as solicitous as he should have been after leaving his supposed friend and a cub in a wood in a historic storm. This time it was lasagna.

Food worried me. Worried me because it didn't worry me: I couldn't duplicate the precariousness of the badger's own life. We did our best: we ate earthworms, both raw and cooked, and any other flotsam tossed up by the valley that we could keep down. We scraped a squirrel off the road and had it with wood sorrel and wild garlic. But there were Meg's regular gifts, which we had neither the discipline nor the churlishness to refuse, and lying guiltily at the bottom of the backpack were sardines, tuna, and beans.

Some later reading helped. Badgers really aren't, usually, neurotically urgent hunters. Starvation is an important cause of death, but mostly among cubs. The choice of earthworms as the staple is a good one. Earthworms are resilient—even to drought. In most English woodlands, most of the time, a significant proportion of the earth's weight is worms. When the topsoil turns to dust, the worms dive and the badgers dig. Dry nights are longer and busier, but although drought affects breeding success (which no doubt makes for an unquiet psyche), it is rarely deadly for individuals. We could have eaten that lasagna less guiltily.

* * *

"It's ridiculous to think that you can know this wood like a badger," said Burt a week or so later. "You can't even know it like me, and a badger knows it like me, but far, far better. We've only been here five hundred years or so, but even so, you'll never catch me up. A man whose DNA has been sloshing round the wood for half a millennium knows more about a badger's world than someone who sniffs and slithers around for a few weeks."

I was annoyed. I was determined to take one part of the wood—the badger's part—from Burt. It shouldn't be hard, I thought. He's just a man. I'm halfway to being a badger.

The first step in any campaign is to know where you are. You need a map. And you need to know what's possible and what's not. That second step was easy. Burt's nose has been devastated by years of roll-ups, and his brain by generations of agricultural reductionism. We'd been in hard olfactory training with lumps of cheese, our noses were a badger's height from the mulch, and we were humble: O so humble. We could quickly overtake his ancestral, generic understanding of the land with our specific olfactory wisdom.

So, over several squirming, scraping, scratching weeks, we made our own map of the wood. It was a scent map, and its contours were very different from the physical ones. When you walk through a town, you see piles of bricks with holes in them, topped with slanting tile and penetrated by pipes. You do a bit of processing and call these things "houses." You do a bit more processing and call them, on account of the shape of the holes or the angle of the tiles, houses of a particular type. From a pile, via an eye, to some sort of Platonic abstraction in a millisecond. After a while our noses began to brew abstractions, too, but using the metaphors encoded deep in our brains by the processing of visual information.

The bracken formed big, emphatic, monolithic blocks— the olfactory equivalent of a grand but gray and uniform housing development. It was too strongly and monotonously aromatic to be satisfying. Better noses than ours would make something of the sparse vegetation around the bracken roots, and even we began, slowly, to be able to see slight differences in the window fittings, the roof angles, and the decorations around the doors.

The oaks—even the small ones—were all determinedly different from each other. They followed the unpatterned pattern of a house I once knew on a plain in East Africa: built with a systematic ramshackleness of grass, mirrors, surfboards, and copies of the *Proceedings of the Linnaean Society*, all cemented with elephant dung and garnished with human bones, diapers, and fragments of Catullus on corkboards.

You'd have thought that trees close to each other would smell alike—or at least more alike than trees far apart. But it wasn't, or wasn't necessarily, so. We could mark our blindfolded crawls from the sett fairly well using just the nearby oaks: "Out of the tunnel, turn right. Fifteen yards; raw tobacco, mostly Turkish; straight on. After half a minute, wall of limes and sick in front. Resolves into oranges rubbed on leather to your left, and mushroom risotto with too much parmesan to your right. Head gently downhill. Flaking saddles with neatsfoot oil somewhere on the shelf. Bear on down for cobwebs and garlic paste."

Individual ashes were similarly distinct, but less emphatically: Arts and Crafts houses somewhere in the Sussex downs. We couldn't distinguish between individual beeches (mansion blocks off the Brompton Road), elders (yellow brick, plastic windows, red asphalt drive for the company car), or alders (row houses in Bradford). ("For God's sake," said Burt. "I used to like metaphors until I met you.")

The more monolithic the blocks, the more fiercely and successfully they fought with other blocks for domination of the valley. The oaks didn't stand a chance: they didn't exist as a block at all. In high summer the bracken generally had the upper hand. When we returned in the autumn, the beeches ruled the wood but were themselves edged out by the elders by the time of the first frost.

To these crude rules there were many exceptions. We were in a seething bottle. Scent sometimes rocketed up from a particular tree and came down in a strange pattern, reaching distant ground before it hit the tree's own shadow. The edges of the wood, and particularly the hedges, seemed olfactorily sterile—or at least hopelessly confusing to scent-hunting predators. They were relatively safe corridors, along which tender, timorous, succulent things crept, invisible to black noses above sharp teeth.

There were tides in the wood, as powerful and predictable as on any beach. As the sun rose, air, and thus scent, was sucked up the side of the valley. The elders moved, like Birnam Wood, through the stands of beech and bracken, and by midday could be found on the lip. They stayed there until nightfall, then slowly retreated back to the river. They were fully back home by three in the morning.

So we made some progress with that scent map. But after a few weeks on my belly in the wood, I despaired. I had an unchangeably visual world. I painted it in shapes and colors, and then added in smell and hearing as extras. Sometimes smell could be powerfully evocative: a smell would pick me up and dump me back into the past with a speed and force that the wraiths of visual memory could never manage. Smell, buried deep in the most ancient part of the brain stem, could petulantly remind me of the sovereignty it had when my ancestors were fish and lizards. Sometimes a voice came first out of my memory. But smell and hearing were always and only the assistants of vision, the great conjuror who brings our worlds out of the hat. No parlor games with cheese and joss sticks could change that. The problem wasn't mainly to do with the sensitivity of my nose; it was about the architecture of my universe. Badgers lived in a universe that wasn't even parallel to mine; it was aligned at an angle to mine that no geometry I knew could coherently describe. So I'll settle for incoherent description.

Consider two examples, both from Ernest Neal's classic book *The Badger*. In the first example, a man placed his palm on a badger path for one minute at 11:00 a.m. At 10:00 p.m. a boar came along the path. He stopped where the palm had been applied, sniffed, and made a detour. A sow who came along at the same time simply wouldn't pass: she took her cubs back to the sett.

And here is my reworking, using the language I learned in the wood.

Along the path there was a wall, built of scent particles

sticking to the veins of dead leaves and the squashed casts of long-dead worms. To the boar, that wall had definite dimensions: he could skirt around the edge and go into the world beyond. For the sow, made conservative and fearful by maternal responsibility, the wall was indefinitely high and long, and the world beyond it unthinkable.

In the second of Neal's examples, a badger path went across a grassy field. The field was plowed up and sown with corn. Badgers took precisely the same route across it.

My reworking: This second path lay between two high but transparent and permeable walls. They each had two dimensions: a physical and a mental. The scent particles that made up the physical part of the walls were tumbled and deep underground, yet they generated a psychic field that rose high into the air above the corn and cut a swath through the badger's brain. The path wove around obstacles that had long since ceased to exist save in the nose-brain-memory.

* * *

An eight-year-old has a plastic nose, and can recover quickly the old knowledge of how to use it. After the first week, as we were watching ladybirds mash aphids, Tom had said: "I can smell mice," and he'd set off along a new path, swimming breaststroke through the grass, his nose grazing the ground. He was very nearly right. He'd smelled and uncovered a network of bank vole runs, marked by droppings, fine chopped stems, and urine. But what was more interesting was how he hunted. He sniffed very fast—several snuffles a second. This, I later learned, is precisely what scent-reliant mammals do. It's called "odor sampling," and it increases the percentage of air that's diverted to the nasal epithelium. Normal efficient breathing sends air direct to the lungs. I tried it; it works dramatically. I now make a different and very unrefined noise at wine tastings.

There's little point in being able to climb neuronally down the evolutionary tree (terrible and terribly constricting vertical language, that) if you're too fastidious to leave the top branches. Tom had mercifully few of my inhibitions. He licked slugs, although medically unwise, I've learned ("The big black ones are a bit bitter, and the bigger they are, the bitterer they are: I prefer the browner ones; they're sort of nutty"), crunched up a grasshopper ("Like prawns that taste of nothing"), had his tongue bitten by a centipede and his nose invaded by ants, and sucked up earthworms like spaghetti ("The big ones are hairy, and I don't like that so much").

It wasn't just his nose that was plastic. All of him inched toward badgerhood. His Achilles tendons stretched and his wrists and neck tightened so he could frolic four-footed through the fern arcades. He swore he could hear a woodpecker's tongue being thrust through holes in tree bark. "I can, you know. Imagine a nail file whispering." (I'm imagining, Tom, and how the hell can we make you go to school to unlearn it?) When the night congealed around the base of the trees, he'd go over and stir the clots of dark with his finger, saying that they swirled and stuck to his hand. His body in the sett or on one of our midday couches seemed to flow around the stones. The wood never stuck into him, as it did into me.

* * *

Most mammals spend a lot of time sleeping. Badgers certainly do, and so did we—much more than usual. We became more tired the more multimodal we became. We should have expected it. We were paying attention to so much more. It's exhausting trying to make sense of lots of voices clamoring for a hearing. Normally, when we're in the countryside, our sight works overtime. Every step on a walk is a completely new and cognitively challenging view. We have never seen before the arrangement of stones upon which our left foot is about to descend; nor that completely different one upon which our right one is about to descend; and so on. To say nothing of the orientation of those leaves on that branch of that tree, in that gust, which have never been that way before in the entire history of the universe, and never will be that way again.

Our "normal" views are in fact deeply abnormal and crushingly dull: those chairs, in that corner of that room. That picture over the mantelpiece—perhaps an ossified version of one tiny fraction of one outdoor second, which nonetheless (it's better than the chairs) eases the retinas designed to catch the millions of utterly different fractions that in fact followed it. The only moment-by-moment visual differences in the lives of most of us are the changing characters on a computer screen, and we don't see those as visual at all: we see straight through them to the abstractions they represent. No wonder our poor starved brains will drink down any change they can get—even if it's the flashing of Simon Cowell's dentistry. Take any of us for the mildest of country walks, and we're immediately in thrilling—but exhausting—sensory overload. We're bombarded with change. Everything demands a response. We have to pay unaccustomed attention. And this, I presume, is why people say that they sleep better after a bit of fresh air.

Now imagine what a wood is like if you're paying attention to what enters not just through your eyes, but also through your ears, your nose, and your skin. And imagine that through each of these portals barges a different world, which maps only mystically onto the others. It's tiring even to think about it. It's exhausting to experience. It takes a lot of processing. So badgers and yogis sleep, and so did we.

Badgers aren't blind: they just don't open their sensory batting with their eyes. Their eyes seem to build a version of the wood composed mostly of shapes. They are silhouette-generators, and their visual memory seems to be concerned mostly with comparing the presently visible silhouette with previous versions. In other words, they're on the lookout mostly for change in the gross structure of the wood. Put the Empire State Building on the ridge and they'd be spooked on Wednesday night and, so long as it didn't change or belch out threatening smells, cautious on Thursday and blasé on Friday.

We can do better than badgers in the day, of course, and even in the gathering dusk we can pick out visual nuances for rather longer than they can. Yet, for most of the time that matters to badgers, we're visually on a level playing field: we're silhouetters. To make use of this skill we need their capacity for the recollection and comparison of successive images. Most of us have this in embryo already. If a very minor change has been made to a familiar room, we'll say: "Something's different." That itself, without more, is useful if you're living in a potentially hostile wood. Even if the change can't be identified, the fact of the change will be enough to keep you underground, away from teeth and claws. But actually badgers seem able, often, to be more specific. They'll note a change, then they'll identify its location by reference to their library of previous images, and then they'll swing their noses and ears onto the target to collect further information.

This demands an intense *localness*—a knowledge of the exact relationship of the individual badger's body in both space and time to the wood. It was this localness, above all, that I wondered if I could acquire. I hoped most desperately that I could.

Alan Garner simply and wonderfully wrote: "On a hill in Cheshire the Garners *are.*" From that fact flowed all his books, all his worlds, all his power. The resonance of that hill is the timbre of Fundindelve, its evenings the fading light of Elidor. I envy Garner enormously his ability to write this sentence. There has never been anywhere that the Fosters *are.*

We have had two strategies to deal with this. The first (my

own) is to try to pretend that we are at home everywhere. This has failed predictably and dramatically. It has resulted in pretension, superficiality, and neurosis. The second (that of most of the rest of my family) is to insist that it doesn't matter that we're not at home wherever we happen to be. This has generated a sort of hereditary lantern-jawed stoicism: we're islands in a wicked sea. But we've never really had any shared characteristics other than the name, and the strategy has not made us thrive. In practice it mainly meant that we watched too much television.

Badgers *belong* to a place, and hence (terribly important, that *hence*) own it, as few or no other animals do. Their hillside dynasties outlive our own most hoarily heraldic, begartered families. Their bodies are built from the recycled earth of a few acres. They burrow deep, and know whatever roams our underworld. They have the connection with a body of land that one can get with any body only by penetration. Their hold on this local life is viciously strong: they're terribly hard to kill or displace. Their skulls are thick. Spades bounce off their sagittal crest. Once they've locked their teeth in the throat of an invading terrier you have to break the jaw to pry them off.

Badgers, for me, are the embodiment of the genius loci.

We don't know of many badger gods from old Europe, but one, Moritasgus (the "Great Badger"), is commemorated in some Gaulish inscriptions from the Côte d'Or. He seems to have been syncretized with Apollo, and thus was regarded mainly as a healing deity. The theology of this association is uncertain, but not hard to guess. When a badger disappears into the earth it is on a shamanic journey. It can, if the ritual is right, carry on its broad shoulders the petitions of the people. It will take them to the Great One, of which it is an acolyte, and if the Great One is pleased to do so, it will send the badger back to the upper world with the transforming blessing.

But, as usual, there are many layers. The root of *tasgus* in "Moritasgus" probably came from the Old Irish *tadg*—one of several words for a poet. (*Tadg* may be preserved in our own modern word *badger*.) Such was the knowledge of the power of words in that world that the functions of poet and shaman, and the meaning of the words for them, tended to merge. Yet the fact that the badger was seen specifically as a word-bearer, a logos-smith, an incantator, is significant. Here's my fancy. The badger carried between the world above and the world below the words that interpreted each side to the other. It enabled each side to make sense of its context, and hence of itself. It shuttled like a sewing machine, stitching the world together; making it whole; giving it an integrity it would otherwise have lacked. And it still does.

If this is possible for a badger, perhaps it is possible for us. Perhaps even for me. Perhaps if we all shuttle enough across frontiers the world won't fall apart.

A few weeks in a wood doesn't make you local. Localness means that you weave around your moldering ancestors. Yet our human lives are so long, and our capacity for skin shedding so great, that we can become our own ancestors. The ground in which the ancestors molder has to be real, not figurative. But we can settle in a place, and by living sufficiently completely to each moment, die completely to each moment, too, so that the place becomes littered with our own corpses, and we can fix our landscapes by reference to their graves. I'm trying to live, and thus to die, on a piece of moorland in Devon, and, thanks partly to the badgers' lessons, I'm making some progress.

Of course we never began to know the wood as Burt did. Over a few centuries you can't help sharing some of your collective unconscious with the dwarf oaks next door. We merge with our neighbors. Every shared breath is an act of copulation in which our DNA gets mingled. ("You, my friend, are one seriously disturbed freak," said Burt.) Yet even in our short time there we started to seep into the wood, and it into us. We noticed that our first slitherings had found, with uncanny canniness, the easiest ways across the landscape from and to our sett. Our prone bodies felt the land, molded it, and were increasingly molded by it. We got calluses where it was good to get them, our legs learned to stretch to slide easily over a fallen beech. We followed these paths religiously and increasingly automatically. Badgers are the same: they have firmly established paths, from which they are very, very reluctant to deviate. These are marked with the scent of badgers who died during the Civil War, and it would take a landslide or a bulldozer to change them.

For all my wilderness fetishism, I found that I wanted the land to bear my mark. Badgers obsessively mark all sorts of objects in their territories with the secretions from their musk glands, and defecate diligently on the borders. I have a less healthy relationship with my own dung, but found that I put my hand repeatedly on the same parts of the same rocks, just to see a reassuring polish. This was my musking. I had to know that *I* had been there. This wasn't a thirst for possession, but a need to confirm that I belonged to the place—that we had shared some continuity. The *I* part was strong. If you take a badger cub and put it in a pen, it'll frantically, incontinently musk. Then it calms down, as if reassured by the smell of itself and the knowledge that it and the pen share some history. It was like that for me.

Karen Blixen, when she was about to leave Kenya, asked: "Will the flowers on the plains of Africa reflect a color that I have worn?" The answer, for her, was no, and there was some sort of self-ablatory salvation in the answer. Andrew Harvey was explicit: "It is the things that ignore us that save us in the end." Blixen's conclusion was wrong. The Ngong Hills were immutably different because she had breathed and worn a red dress among them. And even if she was right, I have to believe that Harvey was wrong. If he got it right, there is no possibility of relationship with anything, and thus no possibility of any sort of salvation. You can't live or die like that. It's that sort of salvation that I was seeking as my hand stretched out to the rock by the beech bole.

* * *

The winter broods over the summer, finding its way into the sunniest August badger. There's a new urgency in the snuffling and rooting once the days shorten. Cereals and fruits are added to the worms and slugs; they're good for fat building.

We, too, know that winters are coming. For many of us it is the ruling fact: the whole year is surrendered to the cold. The thoughts and itineraries of the summer are the lackeys of the dark.

I fight hard against this demonic capitulation, but it is hard to enjoy an August day qua August day. The stronger the fight, the greater the acknowledgment of the eventual defeat. I race around, like the badgers, manically soaking up the heat. The greater the mania, the greater the depression that follows. It shouldn't be like this: I should be able to live in January as a smug, torpid parasite on the body of July. That's what the badgers do. They don't hibernate, but there's not much in the diary from November to March apart from sleep, the occasional sortie for worms, stretching and a change of air, and gestation.

There's a week in early May, after the Green Man has been piped and caroled back, when the world seems all right, when resurrection rules, and it's possible to believe that resurrection is the rule. But this faith fades fast. By mid-June, when we were first in the sett, the liquid sun of the blackcap's call starts to sound like a taunt ("It'll soon be gone, soon be gone, it will"), and its name ominous.

* * *

I chewed, gagged, sniffed, and waddled my way toward the badger's world. Sometimes I felt that I came near, only to find that the conceit of that feeling meant I was farther away than ever. We heard the real badgers every night as they crashed through the bracken, and occasionally got a flash of head stripes in the dusk, or a darkening of a shadow as a badger lumbered into it. We'd often try to approach them, and got good at hearing them pause, then putting their fears to rest by loudly scratching ourselves. We put our front paws on trees and stretched as soon as we came out of our hole. We defecated on mounds chosen for their view of the hill. We acquired a thick patina of scent that even Burt, his nose full of lanolin and diesel, could know and resent. When Tom was ahead of me, in warm, damp weather, I could pick up his vapor trail for twenty minutes.

Burt's jibes and meals became less frequent. We were left on our own to be encrusted by the valley. We saw strange lights in a long-abandoned house. Our hackles rose when we heard farm dogs. Distant figures in nylon were as far away as the moon, and a good deal less relevant. We cared about the weight of the clouds, the color of the leaves, and the hunger of the midges. We put a badger's skull on a stick outside the sett for no reason I can identify clearly. We washed very occasionally, and even then patchily. Our mouths tasted of mud and smoke. A wren speared a caterpillar on Tom's leg as he lay snoring in a clump of dead bluebells. My watch seemed offensive: I took it off, put it in a plastic bag, and ceremonially buried it. We stood at attention. I played the Last Post on my tin whistle.

And, for that summer, we had to be content with that: had to be satisfied with knowing that in some ways, perhaps for a few minutes, we had lived in the same place as some badgers. That's all we thought we'd done.

* * *

I dug up the watch. We went back to Abergavenny Station thinking that we'd failed—that the Puck of otherness had dodged away, as usual, away into the murmuring greenwood.

The town blared, belched, leered, and cackled. There was more variegation on one leaf outside our sett than there was in the whole place. It fed itself by oriental air freight, and everyone was the same color. They talked about the adulteries of footballers and tone-deaf singers. The scent blocks were huge and crass; they lurched and swung and bellowed. I felt sick from shock and boredom and the heaving floors of deafening smell. Someone asked me the way to the ATM. It seemed as if he was shouting at the top of his voice, nose to mine. I jumped through the roof and nearly knocked him down. And yet, as an example of a human settlement, this is one of the very best. I've always been happy there.

I was desperate to get back to the valley. On the train I put in earplugs and looked out at the fields sliding past—the distances hideously shortened by the engine. Then I took out the earplugs and put on the calls of the woodland birds. I was missing something that I very urgently needed—something I had recently had.

So here is the first proposition: to thrive as a human being, I needed to be more of a badger.

* * *

Back home I forgot a lot very quickly. But, though my nose returned to its usual inertia, and I became used again to the tinnitus that we call normal living, it wasn't all lost. I had the dreamy tetchiness of the exile. I knew that it was possible, as a matter of sensory routine rather than yogic contortion, to pay attention to the world in many planes at once rather than just our usual one or two, and something of what there is to be perceived when you do.

Tom and I went back to the sett in midwinter. There were cobwebs over the mouth, which was rather hurtful. I'd hoped that it would be adopted, at least by foxes. The badger skull was still on the stick, but its position had shifted, so that instead of staring at the ground it looked up the hill, through the cracking old man's fingers of the oaks, past the silent rookery, to the house that Burt had built that summer, where Meg was mulling cider, reading the Mabinogion, and calmly ignoring the epidemic of diarrhea and vomiting that had felled all the children.

Our paths were still there, just about. They'd be gone by the spring, but they would still be the best way through the wood if you were crawling. When you lay on the ground an aching cold, the color of mourning, cascaded in, starting with the ribs, filling the chest, and streaming down to the legs. The ground seemed hungry for us: it sucked and nibbled.

Outside the brown thickets of dripping bracken, the wood was bigger to the eyes, and sight much more relevant than it had been in the summer. There were sometimes clear horizons, and often distinct trees. Winter gives badgers distance. But it takes away that succulent marriage with the earth that is brokered by noses and summer heat. The thin winter sun worked hard but (for us) vainly to smash the ground into grains we could smell. There was leaf mold and inchoate decay, and that was all. The winter wood was flat, much more like ours than the summer wood had been.

Ears came into their own. The longer sight lines meant that our ears could focus on sounds from distant objects, and since there wasn't so much going on, they could give a much fuller report on each sound now than they could in the humming summer.

The real badgers of the wood were quiet, but about. There was fresh dung in their lavatories, gray and white hairs on the barbed wire, and pad marks in the mud on their highways. We heard them puffing along in the night like old shunters in a rail roach yard, out of condition. They should have felt close: their snorting was unbaffled by the thick green of June; the clear air had only to carry the call of a tentative tawny owl rather than the thrum and thrust and shrill of the summer. But they seemed farther away than ever: we shared less; it seemed they had less to share, or that they were less willing than in generous June.

The sett closed coldly around us. This time its walls were jaws. The worms liked the heat that leached and was leeched out of us. They came, like hairy tongues from the jaws, and slimed over us.

"I don't like this," whimpered Tom, shivering in a sleeping bag that was far too thin. "Neither do I," said I. "Let's go." So we gathered up our stuff and went across the river, up a track that was straighter in the moonlight than in the noonlight, and back to the farm.

No badgers came out to salute us. They were warm. Their sett was much deeper in the wood than ours; far deeper than we could safely go.

3. OTTER

Every morning five otters watch us having breakfast. They are dead Victorian otters, bleached white by the taxidermist in the manner of the day, looking haughtily out like cavalry colonels, their feet on vanquished fish. The Victorians wanted white otters, and so they got them. We all tend to get the otters we want. They are tools, in a way that few other species are. Henry Williamson (*Tarka the Otter*) figuratively mashed up his otters and used the paste to paint north Devon, and to smear as balm on the wounds, real and imaginary, left by the trenches. Gavin Maxwell (*Ring of Bright Water*) wanted, and therefore got, rollicking, boisterous otter friends who wouldn't ask him too much about himself and could be cuddled on lonely Hebridean nights. I have only this advantage over those true masters of otter writing: I don't like otters very much.

Being an otter is like being on speed. In suburban life the nearest I can legally get to it is to stay up for a couple of nights, drinking a double espresso every couple of hours, before having a cold bath followed by a huge breakfast of still-twitching sushi and then a nap, and then keep repeating until I die—which I would do most authentically by running in front of a car, or from septicemia from an abdominal wound.

Writing about otters is, more than for any other animal, an accountancy exercise. They are metabolic businesses running with very tight margins. They spend more than three quarters of their lives asleep. That's more than eighteen hours a day. The remaining six hours are spent in frenetic killing.

They have a resting metabolism about 40 percent higher than animals of comparable size. That rises massively when they're swimming, particularly in cold water. A swimming otter's metabolic motor is running at around four and a half times the speed of a dog's. It doesn't quite work like this, but imagine your dog's heartbeat jumping to five times its exercising rate. The chest wouldn't really thump: it would flutter as if a huge hummingbird were caged inside it. An engine like that needs an unfeasible amount of fuel—around 20 percent of the otter's body weight each day.

I'm around 15 stone—95 kg. If we go just by the weight of food, to keep up with the otter's intake, each day I'd have to eat about eighty-eight Big Macs (all three tiers, with both patties, cheese, iceberg lettuce, pickles, onions, and that strange pink sauce). Or 3,800 standard bags of potato chips, 229 regular cans of baked beans, or around 792 lamb chops or fishcakes. Eighty-eight Big Macs in six waking hours is around fifteen per hour, or one every four minutes. It's no wonder that otters never look as if they have time for reflection.

Otters are made sinuous only by physics. There are many poems celebrating their lubricity, but these are celebrations of the water, not the animal. Otters are spiky things. We want something to flow with its environment, for some reason about which we can wax all metaphysical. But otters won't do it. We talk about flow and laminae; we should talk about bristle and snap and scrabble. They are invaders, not citizens. They shove those winsome little noses between the laminae like surgically gloved fingers pushing inside an orifice. They are wedges, splitting up the river. They turn fish away from the flow and crush them. They hardly belong in the water. They've not been there long enough to be the foundational-mythical water animals we want them to be. It's been only about 7 million years or so.

They are land animals who dabble, impressively but precariously, in the water. They're much more stoat than seal. Evolution has only just begun to tinker with these primordial stoats, flattening their skulls, shifting their eyes and nostrils to slightly more advantageous positions, and giving them thicker coats, tails like hairy outboard motors, and some half-hearted webbing between their toes. And with those modest bequests, evolution threw otters into the deep, cold end and told them to get on with it, tyrannized by horrific thermodynamic arithmetic.

The arithmetic makes them wanderers. In a warm, fecund lowland river an otter might be able to run on the fuel it finds in six miles or so of water. In leaner Scotland it might need to cover thirty. The numbers also make them vicious: lose a fish to an invader and the balance sheet starts to look scary. Too scary, most of the time, for playful niceties. More than half of the dead otters autopsied have been in recent fights. The injuries are typically very unpleasant: otters fighting in water go for the underbelly and the genitalia. Bellies are unzipped and guts unraveled; testicles are ripped off, penises snapped. And that's not the worst of it. We don't see the worst injuries: they must kill the otters quickly, leaving them stiff in a bankside bush for the rats, or at the bottom of a pool for the scavenging fish. We see otters only when they survive long enough to be hit by a van.

What can I do to get close to these jangling, snarling, roaming, twitching bundles of ADHD, other than acknowledge that, like them, I'm a pretty shabby evolutionary compromise with a short attention span, poised on the edge of an onto-logic precipice? Well, I can start by getting to where they are, and when I'm there resetting the physical boundaries of my world so that they coincide with the otters'. This, to begin with, is a matter of pins in maps.

At the center of our map is a little gray cottage on the edge of a moor in Devon. If you climb through the bracken to the top of the hill you look over the Bristol Channel to the throbbing lights of Wales. Herring gulls tug ticks from the anuses of red deer. We pull our water from the stream that runs past the cottage. The stream slices through badger woods, picking up speed and oak leaves, and coating the stones with peat as if they've been dipped in a chocolate fondue. Mysteriously it slows down just before it meets the East Lyn River, as if it is having second thoughts about leaving the hill: it weeps resentfully under the road and is bowled off to Lynmouth for lobster and chips.

But with us it is a cheery little river. It pauses and pools. There are chiff-chaffs, toad nurseries, and algal fans like lace doilies. Our hill is a strong, rosy-cheeked bit of moorland that throws its weight around. The caddis fly larvae use boulders, not grains, in their coats. But beware of thinking it's all simple and bucolically beery. There's a stand of tortured trees sprawling and sucking like mangroves. The children won't go in without leaving limpet shells as propitiatory gifts for whatever sleeps on the hammocks of moss.

At the very top of the valley, three minutes from our kitchen table, just as the river leaks off the moor, there was, as an act of grace, an otter spraint.

Otters use sprainting (depositing dung) as a way of saying "This is my patch," or "This pool has just been fished: don't waste time here." It may not be their only remote method of territorial signaling (urine might be important, and there's a gratifyingly vigorous debate about the significance of "anal jelly," a rich, marmalade-like substance that probably eases the passage of sharp fish bones through vulnerable gut). But it is certainly the most visible. Indeed, it is usually the only sign that there are otters around, but spraint study has badly distorted our understanding of their biology. It has been truly said that we study spraint, not otters.

Spraint's a merry specialty. Its professors shamble happily along riverbanks with their clipboards, charting, extrapolating, and eating cheese and pickle sandwiches. But it's rather vain. Shit just won't bear the scientific edifices we purport to build on it. You can't reconstruct my life from my stools.

Dung is good for some things, though. You'd expect the otter's bowel habits to reflect its extraordinary metabolic rate. And indeed it does. Hans Kruuk devotedly monitored sprainting behavior in Shetland. In winter, when sprainting is much commoner than in the summer, he recorded about three spraints per hour. And that was just spraints—deposit on the riverbank—rather than episodes of defecation. He must have missed some spraints, and even more evacuations— some of which must have happened in the water. Assuming six hours of waking time, and thus sprainting time per day, that's eighteen spraints a day. That's a lot of signaling. Those are busily conversational bowels. Assuming one and a half bowel movements per child per day, an otter can mark in a day what it would take each of my children twelve days to do.

I gave the children a little lecture on sprainting, then sent them off up the valley. "Spraint," I said. "But don't fall in, and be back for supper."

It was a failure, of course. Human children can't produce bowel movements to order, and to give them laxatives with the Rice Krispies just for the purpose of this book would be at least unkind, and possibly illegal. So I changed the instruction. "Whenever you need to go, go up the river and choose a place. It must say: this part of the river is mine."

Out went the children. They instinctively mimicked the sprainting behavior of European otters, choosing exactly the same exposed, strategic stones that otters would have used. When there were no stones, they even created, just as otters do, "castles"—little grass or sand platforms on which to display their spraints, as engagement rings are displayed on velvet cushions.

The next thing was to see how distinctive each spraint was—how emphatically it declared its origins. This was a revolting job, and it must have looked deeply perverted. We crawled up the river, sniffing.

The results were surprising. Our children have identical diets, but they produced very different feces. It wouldn't be kind to match the type of stool to the name. So I'll just say that A is the outlier: he must metabolize his bile salts in a very eccentric way. B is placenta and balsamic. And so on. We did blind sniffings: all five of us (my wife stayed fastidiously inside, optimistically reading about gracious living in a glossy magazine) were right about 80 percent of the time.

That was with fresh dung. Sun baking rapidly reduced our accuracy. So did low temperatures. It was what we'd found in the scent world of the badger. After a week, in any conditions, dung was simply dung, and we'd have to resprint if we wanted to say anything with it. Otters do the same: the chain of signals is constantly eroded by the rain, the sun, and rising water, and is diligently reforged, usually immediately before or immediately after a meal.

Our sprainting told us (for a while) who had been on the river, and where they had decided to make their mark. C, tiny and tentative, had a correspondingly tiny territory. D made little scatological shrines around a single pool, every offering nestling under arches of fern or reed. A and B, colonially aggressive, sought to extend their own territories far up onto the moor, and to annex the other's. They hunted down each other's spraints and kicked them into the river, substituting theirs, or crowingly topped the rival spraint with one of theirs.

If we fed our children more distinctive food than we do, we'd have been able to reconstruct the meals of eight hours ago. But all this information amounts to very little. Those spraints hardly say much about the lives of either the individual children or human children generically. A lot of published otter biology is, literally, shit.

* * *

I was having far too good a time. Having a good time was inauthentic. Otters don't. At least not in these hard-pressed days. They jangle fearfully from fish to fight, never sure how the figures are going to stack up when the latest bellyful of bone and slime has passed on. Henry Williamson tells us, so emphatically that it's in the subtitle, that *Tarka the Otter* is about Tarka's "Joyful Water-Life and Death." If Williamson was right, Tarka was an unusually, pathologically euphoric otter. There are joyful badgers, deer, and swifts. Lots of them. But few constitutionally joyful otters. They don't have time for emotional fripperies. To be a perpetual hunter, in an economy like ours and theirs, is to be perpetually hunted. And that's what you see: in their time sheets, their little cold eyes, and their corticosteroid levels.

Otters don't have horizons other than the level of the water. They are furry worms, and there's no point in them seeing far. They bore tunnels through the river and the sea and kill things in those tunnels as moles kill worms. They live in their tunnels. It is psychologically apt that they should. When humans are—no, when I am—consumed with the anxiety that reflects the way the otter has to live, I, too, am in a tunnel, visually suffocated. I stand higher off the ground than an otter, but I see just as little. I might be walking through the Renaissance gallery in the Ashmolean, but I might as well be wriggling through wet cow parsley on a riverbank, my eyes full of rain and my nostrils full of the assurance of death. Even my distractions, which a naive biologist might think are evidence of playful hedonia, are failed attempts to break out of the pain. The biologist would see the attempt; he wouldn't see the failure. I play with my children in the unbelieving hope that they might be unlike me, and so might be spared the tunnel.

Otters bend. They can look up. But when they do, they see the rising bank ahead, washed with green, or the hairy teeth of nettles, or an ash arch, or a slug oozing over a burdock ceiling. They know the sky is there, but they do not watch it. Their country brushes against their flanks and slowly unfurls at the pace of a paw strike: it does not leap or roll as ours does. There are no steep valleys, because nothing is steep if it is taken at that height and pace. There are no prolonged ascents or descents in an otter's life, because there is no prolonged anything. These animals inhabit the instant, but not in a way that epiphanically redeems it. There is a wretched, desperate, hypertensive, hungry moment. Then there is another such moment. And another. The dots are not connected, in that flattened head, to form a personality. Anxiety, when it is severe, erodes the self. If it is constitutional it precludes a self. Otters are circuit boards. There's nothing else there.

C. S. Lewis thought that animal suffering wasn't as worrying an indictment of the goodness and/or omnipotence of God as one might imagine, because in order to suffer properly, as we do, you've got to know that the noxious neuronal storm at point A in time is connected to the neuronal storm at point B, and hence is likely to persist, noxiously, into point C. A lot of the angst is in the extrapolation and the attendant unpleasant anticipation. Animals, lacking the conviction of an *I* that's the subject of pain, and, in any event, lacking the neuronal hardware to extrapolate a present nasty sensation into a troubling conviction of a future one, don't suffer.

I've always thought that this was nonsense, and I still do. But I come nearest to believing it in the case of those manic otters, too consumed by their desire to consume to have anything spare for the construction of a self.

How do I know this about otters? I don't, of course. It has no neurobiological basis at all. It is deeply unscientific to come over all Beatrix Pottery with badgers but deny to their very close cousins, the otters, even the ability to feel pain. But I can't help my intuition. And I don't apologize for it much.

I'm very surprised to be writing such terrible things about otters. I used to love them uncritically and sentimentally. I took a toy otter to bed for years, and mortgaged a Lego set to buy a stuffed one from a junk shop in Glastonbury. I stroked the real one's scarred muzzle as I sank into sleep, thinking that the scars came from the hounds and that I could make it posthumously better. I still like many of the things that go with otters—all the things that people write poems about. I am glad that their bodies, though as big as fat foxes', can flutter like gut weed in a gust of water; that they can turn on themselves like paper clips; that they whicker and whistle, and that their noses twitch as if they're always flicking off a horsefly. I like their occasional capacity for patience, the appearance of big, happy family outings, and the fact that they curl up in the day in the sort of places I always went when I was on the run from piano practice. I agree with them about the best places to live, and share their disdain for canalization, fertilizer, and fences. They make a good show of personality. But I'm no longer convinced. There's less in a brown head under water than in a black-and-white striped head under earth. Otters suffer less than badgers, foxes, or dogs. And I have betrayed my childhood.

Otters made me wander. Otters themselves have always wandered. Williamson has Tarka ranging over the whole of the land of the rivers Taw and Torridge—a truly epic Bedouin life, if it's true.

Williamson was writing in the 1920s, when West Country rivers were still happy, seething places. Since then we have devastated our rivers with pyrethroids and polychlorinated biphenyls (PCBs) and other nasty things with benzene rings in them. In particular, we've annihilated the eels that are the otter's preferred food. They're around 80 percent of an ideal otter diet, and their numbers are down by about 95 percent.

I doubt that Tarka really undulated throughout the land of the two rivers. If he did, it wasn't because he had to, but because he wanted to: there are, no doubt, otters like that, just as there are people like that. But it would be surprising if a modern-day Tarka didn't roam much farther than his early-twentieth-century ancestors: the fish pickings per mile are much leaner.

The benzene rings make otters cross moors, watersheds, and, dangerously, roads and the paths of other otters. Hunger breeds aggression: those disembowelings and castrations can be traced to a human hunger to increase shareholders' profits.

The shareholders, too, have made otters more visible than they were. Otters prefer to hunt at night, but, as generations of hard-pressed humans have found, if you can't make ends meet by working normal hours, you have to moonlight—or, in the otter's case, sunlight. To the stern injunctions of the otter's own physiological accountants—those accountants who keep the metabolism running on such tight margins—are added the crushing demands of the actual besuited accountants in Frankfurt boardrooms, who squeeze things even more tightly, and make highly strung animals strung to the point of snapping; who snatch otters' sleep; who make otters less local.

Otters hold big maps in those small heads. This is a surprise. You'd expect maps that big to go with a more sedate, chugging, philosophical pace. They are maps not just of space but of time, colored by memories of panic, satiety, and loss. My own map says: "The river runs through a steep gorge. On the north side, deciduous trees rise steeply to a plateau, and a stream cuts through them to meet the river a quarter of a mile from the pub. On the south side there's mixed woodland." And my experience and intuition add: "Rachel cut her knee going down there, and she screamed so loudly that the wood, which had buzzed and whistled, was silent for an hour. Then we climbed to the pub, and you can get steak and kidney pie from noon." The otter's map is, as we'd now expect, more like a spreadsheet or a to-do list. It's abrupt, prosaic, and light on adjectives and adverbs. It's divided rigidly by season. It looks like this:

Month	Option 1	Option 2	Option 3	Option 4
January	Eel: deep and dark. Try lower Rockford pools.	Gudgeon, miller's-thumb, and stone loach below Rosborough Castle.	Ducks, moorhens, coots: Try Leeford for dozy ducks. Might be worth the trek to the Barle, or the pool at Radworthy.	Whatever.
February	Eel: deep and dark. God knows. Everywhere's as bad as everywhere else. OK upstream of Brendon 2 years ago, but remember sunken barbed wire and human with exploding stick.	Gudgeon, miller's-thumb, and stone loach: Smallcombe Bridge.	Ducks, moorhens, coots: as for January.	Whatever.
March	Eel: Try Simonsbath bridge. Rats there—good for garnish.	The usual: Holcombe Burrows.	That carp pond. Nasty dog, though.	Whatever.
April	Eel: Maybe Cherrybridge, but it smelled of diesel last January.	Frogs at Shilstone. Worth looking for dead sheep in the stream while there.	Little things at Holcombe Water. And the start of the poultry season.	Whatever.

Month	Option 1	Option 2	Option 3	Option 4
May	Eel: Roots under Flexbarrow.	Spawning river lampreys. Male attached to female's head with sucker and bodies entwined. Two for the price of one. And dead and dying after spawning. Try lower Barle.	Ducklings. Get mother, too, if she argues.	Whatever.
June	Eel: Where Great Woolcombe meets the Barle.	Sea bass: kelp forest off Lynmouth.	Signal crayfish: Barle. Small stuff en route.	Whatever.
July	Eel: Just upstream of Cornham Ford.	Trout: corner, don't chase. Perhaps under Tom's Hill?	Signal crayfish: Barle. Small stuff en route.	Whatever.
August	Eel: If rain, Balewater. If not: just down from Brightworthy.	Trout: corner, don't chase. Wasn't too bad by Cloud Farm last year.	Signal crayfish: Barle. Small stuff en route.	Whatever.
September	Eel: Perhaps Hoar Oak Water?	River lamprey migration. Kill in Watersmeet shallows.	Signal crayfish: Barle. Small stuff en route.	Whatever.
October	If river high, and especially if new moon, possible silver eel migration. Wait just below Watersmeet. Kill in shallows.	River lamprey migration. Kill in Watersmeet shallows.	Signal crayfish: Barle. Small stuff en route.	Whatever.
November	If river high, and especially if new moon, possible silver eel migration. Wait just below Watersmeet. Kill in shallows.	Start month with lampreys: possibly by Ash Bridge. End month with dead and dying just-spawned salmon: Rockford pools.	Signal crayfish: Barle. Small stuff en route.	Whatever.
December	Eel: Myrtleberry Cleave? But nasty there if there's been rain on the moor.	Start month with dead and dying just-spawned salmon: Rockford pools.	Shore crabs, birds, fish junk, crayfish. That pike under the alders. Earthworms after rain. Yes, it's come to that.	Whatever.

Except that a real otter's syntax is less flowery and literary than that in the table.

I can make my mind, and so my language, work like that. I've done it. It involved several days of sleeplessness, a disastrously re-re-re-reforged relationship that had been characterized by years of mutual laceration, three days of cold rain, three days of fasting, a lost tent pole, and a badly stubbed toe. The process would be speeded up by any of the traditional techniques of psychological attrition: white noise, water dripping slowly onto the head, daytime TV, or commercial radio. It would be helpful, too, to have done something irreparably bad, and so to have nothing to lose and nowhere to hide.

I decided to be a relatively relaxed, pre-PCB otter, traveling by night. But you can't start at night. You have to get to know the river by day. Health and Safety, and all that. This is a great shame. It means that the night river—the otter's real river—will always be described by reference to the day. The day is primary. References and comparisons always distort. This puts the otter behind yet another swath of gauze, as if it weren't indistinct enough. But there's no way around it, particularly if you take kids with you, as I sometimes did, and they've got a caring mother who can conjure apocalypse out of the kind air of the Lyn Valley.

But mostly I was alone, because otters are. The popular picture is of cubs romping alongside the bitch. That indeed happens, for about a year. It has to, because the river is unreliable. In February one pool might feed a family, in May it'll be empty. The cubs can't intuit that there will be frogs in an area of swamp in April and exhausted, easily caught cock salmon after the spawning in December. A whole year of systematic and geographically wide-ranging education is necessary. Failure to attend one class could well be fatal.

But this sociability isn't the norm. It is very costly for the bitch. She wants to stop paying those crippling metabolic school bills as soon as she can. Most otters, most of the time, are alone. They have to be. Our sickly rivers aren't fecund enough for sociability. One pool, at one time, might feed one; it won't feed two.

So most of the time, my own cubs rampaged around the cottage, destroying furniture and reenacting the Cain and Abel story, while my wife screamed and despaired, and I let the river take me.

* * *

I have swum the rivers of Exmoor for years, generally by day, usually without a wet suit, and often with a mask and snorkel. But my expression "the rivers of Exmoor" is grand, flabby, and meaningless. You can never step twice into the same river, observed Heraclitus. Quite right: and you can only ever describe one momentary sense impression in one brain. The connections between those impressions are delusory. Yet to make coherent prose, we rely on those delusions: the delusions make for readability, tone, and mood.

If a director were making a film about the valley of the East Lyn, she'd pick, for the background music, something between Debussy at his most anodyne and Wagner at his most hysterical. She'd generalize; she'd have a small set of categories: fierce, Arcadian, and (to show she was sophisticated) ambiguous. She'd never get the speed of the transitions right: the river can lurch between fierce and Arcadian in ten minutes, and it is always ambiguous. But the otter, which seems to inhabit the river, and (despite being an evolutionary newcomer to the water) in a way does, has a different set of cadences altogether; it's far more garage band: fingernails down the musical blackboard. It clashes painfully with the director's categories. Which all goes to show that generalizations are nonsense; that anyone who tries to evoke the mood of a natural place is a fraud; that it is all—all—in the particular; the detail; the slash, the wrench, the individual panting breath, followed by the next individual pant; the little flickers of consciousness coaxed by memory out of the tiny brain of a whistling, bristling, undulating little bastard wedged by the rush of evolution between the water and the wood.

Direction is mysterious. When an otter moves its head down beneath the surface it is really climbing up: it suddenly acquires height. It's immediately on a summit, looking down. The moment before, there was just foreground, the shuddering hide of the water. That slight move of the head doesn't just change the view: it multiplies the dimensions in which it is possible to live. A pit in the riverbed is a peak: as it hunts trout in the pit, the otter treks along a path cut in negative space.

A river is a landscape, with its own storms and shades and holes. Out of the eye of a water wind in the Badgworthy Water, below a magpie's nest, there is a column of absolute still. Move sideways an inch, and you'll be spun away and down, faster than the magpie's flight, onto the rocks where an old ewe has been pinned for years. She had an eel caged in her ribs, fat and complacent as a hunting farmer in a timber-framed house. I came up behind, one February day, shoved a garden fork up where the ewe's diaphragm used to heave, and pulled him thrashing to the bank. While I was feeling strong and manly he bit me in the bollocks and snaked away back to the Eocene.

Just below the sheep pool, in the river-that-momentarily-*is*-but-never-was-and-never-will-be, is a sharp rock staircase that leads down beneath the rolling deck of water to a cave where the river is slow circling syrup. The cave keeps for itself a cache of sycamore keys. Nothing else. They spin up inside the cave, and then they spin down. And then they spin up. And so on, until they rot.

Just downstream of the staircase the moor bleeds into the river. A red earth cloud billows out like blood in a pub toilet after a fight. When you're lying on the riverbed, looking up from underneath the stain on a bright day, the red earth and the blue sky mix on your retina's palette into an episcopal purple.

If a newly dipped sheep walks chest high into the water to drink, everything downstream for fifty yards will die. If the day's hot and it goes farther in to cool off, it'll clear the river for half a mile.

There's a ford. There are sometimes otter tracks and spraint there. Coaches carrying crinolined ladies used to lurch and rumble through it, and it was the ideal place for a lazy highwayman. The shallowness of the river must have caused a lot of robberies, which no doubt caused a hanging or two, which no doubt caused all sorts of other things, including the incubation of many blowfly larvae in the corpse on the gibbet; and no doubt some of the descendants of those blowflies have been slung on hooks to catch the fish of Exmoor.

All of which is to say that the river is a stream of stories, and stories have no beginning and no end. It's in this stream of stories that otters hunt, and into it that I went after them.

* * *

I'm always *after* them. Always looking at faint tracks on a patch of mud or a sandbank; always sniffing at little piles of dung; always looking at an old dead fish with its liver sucked out like a milkshake through a hole behind the gills. I've never been ahead of them, or with them. Sometimes I've had, for a whole moment at a time, the laughable conceit that I've ambushed them: that I've got there before them, and they've walked in on the stage that I built. But no: they're seen only when they choose to be seen. I resent this very much. They give nothing—not even the delusion of companionability. Otters deny reciprocity even more shockingly than cats. It's even more disturbing than their wiredness, or their sleepless, trembling, thirsty killing.

After them into the water I went.

It's important to be in the water a long time. An experience of anything for ten minutes is not qualitatively the same as an experience of an hour. Neurobiological arithmetic is odd. The difference between twenty minutes and ten minutes is not ten minutes. If you don't believe me, get up early in the morning and sit cross-legged on a cushion, with your eyes shut, trying to think of nothing: pick up each intruding thought between your finger and thumb and sling it out of your mind. Do it every morning for three months. Then tell me that ten minutes plus ten minutes is twenty minutes.

Which is why, despite all my macho posturing and all my subcutaneous fat, I tended to wear a wet suit. A good case can be made for the wretched things on other grounds, too. Otters, unlike me, have very little fat, but they have instead two layers of hair: a fine under-layer and a coarse outer coat. They trap air very effectively, and air is an appalling conductor of heat, and thus an excellent insulator. Wet suits work in a similar way. Most of their insulation comes from nitrogen bubbles trapped in the neoprene. It's more otterlike, not less, to wear one.

* * *

The days were easy: I plunged in and drifted down, face-first, pausing to nudge and grope.

But for a lot of the day, like the otters, I lay up near the water. At first, before I discovered the river night, I lay up so that I could hear and smell and see what was in the otter's day. Later, when I began to know the night, I lay up because I was tired from the previous night in the river, and I wanted all my senses to work properly when the sun dissolved in the water and the real show started.

Otters have many favorite lying-up spots. They have to, with such large territories. They're not particularly fussy. Their needs are mine. They want somewhere dry, safe, and, ideally, quiet. They don't need a vaulted ancestral palace under an ancient ash. A drainpipe will do, or a shaded couch of stranded drift grass out of the reach of lolloping dogs. I've slept in a pipe, too, dumped outside Rochester by a contractor, full of rabbit bones, used diapers, and syringes. A bull terrier waddled in, looking for trouble. I snarled and nearly bit his head off. I hope he's in therapy forever. But usually I curled up within a stone's throw of the river, listening with the one waking ear, resenting the gossiping hikers, looking for the night.

In my mind the river has two seasons: light and darkness, life and death. Spring and autumn are desperate, Manichaean battle grounds. The summer breathes and throbs. The winter does not: The heart of the world stops. The world doesn't even wheeze.

In the light I splashed and smiled and bobbed bum-bruisingly down the rapids. The river had wildly varying moods, but they were always moods that went with its age.

Wherever you are, though, when there is sun the bottom of the river is a mosaic of smashed faces, all cackling at each other in a cubist hell. In the young, chatty upper reaches the weed tops those faces with the hair of madwomen in wind. I combed their hair with cold fingers. Loaches hung there like lice.

In the middle age of the river the faces flatten for a while, the hair recedes, and the voice, though never lugubrious, sometimes pauses so that the river can draw breath. Then, before the final few furlongs to the sea, it is menopausal, disgraceful crisis: Ruskin on acid; all hanging greenery; soft focus from the spray—it's too much; it's desperate to make the most of those last few miles of Devon. And then, when you can hear the cough and grumble of surf, it gets measured and reflective. It paces itself.

Wherever you are, most of the daytime life, most of the time, is at the edges, under cover. The visible riverbed is a desert. There are occasional bold caravans across the interior, from rock to rock. Minnow shoals shiver; miller's-thumbs stab and grind. Brown trout, big enough to be complacent, wave with the weed, as a camel sways and cuds in hot sand. Beneath the rock eaves are thousands of eyes the color of the gravel, patient for the dark.

Only occasionally does the day desert bloom. I was in the middle of a bloom once: a mayfly hatch on a June day after a beery lunch at the Staghunters' Inn.

From a distance the mayflies were like the breath of the river. In fact they had been breathed by the river. The surface of the pool was a shivering skin of flesh. I didn't bother to undress. There were too many walkers, and anyway, I'd been sleeping in my clothes for a couple of weeks and they needed a wash. I took off my boots, hung my jacket on a branch, and tobogganed headfirst down a mud slide into the water. I came up with my head in the cloud of flies. This was no amorphous cloud of being: it was a highly organized traffic system. The mayflies yo-yoed just above the ripples—ripples as big for them as the mightier Hawaiian breakers are for the butchest of big-wave surfers. There were rigid corridors above the river, and down each of them raced, like disciplined rush hour freeway traffic keeping to the right lane, five thousand flies a second. I lay for an hour with my head in the central reservation. When I moved my head into one of the carriageways, flies from one direction filled my mouth and eyes; flies from the other piled up gently into the back of my head. An hour after exhaling them, the river inhaled the mayflies back. I didn't know whether to cheer or weep at the wantonness.

Brown trout, which usually hung in the shadows when I joined them in the water, loved the killing more than they hated the floundering of my corduroyed legs and check-shirted arms, and they jabbed past me on the way to the surface like sharp-elbowed matrons en route to the buffet at a wake after an overlong funeral. The mayflies made a roof of steak for the trout's world. Imagine that your ceiling suddenly turned into a hamburger. It would turn your head, and it turned the fishes' heads: they stabbed through the hamburger roof into the air.

Somewhere among the wild garlic, hunched and watching, was a big dog otter, its feet twitching with frustration. Fish as drunk on death as those trout were themselves killable, but here was a fat human thrashing the pool dry. I felt his resentment, sour in the sun. I've never felt anything else from an otter.

When I dragged myself back up the mud slide and shook myself off on the bank, I found that someone had nicked my jacket. I wish them luck: I'm amazed and flattered that they could stomach the smell. Unsurprisingly they couldn't face the boots. I slouched drippingly back up the hill for supper. As I was tucking into the moussaka, the mayfly bodies that the trout were too gorged to take were being churned into protein cream by surf on the Lynmouth rocks.

Usually, though, the light-days in the water were unbiological, unteeming times. I cruised at altitude; surveying, collecting coordinates; the days marked by the click of my scanning shutter eyes rather than the snap of jaws, and the assembling of images into a crude mosaic rather than the dismembering of animal bodies.

We picnicked, played cricket on the riverbank with stones as balls and deer femurs as bats, slept in the shallows, consecrated and defended our own spraining sites, compared (and tasted) the types of maggots that eat fish and those that eat birds and mammals, ate lots of raw fish liver, had (for a week) a rule that we couldn't drink cider unless and until we'd seen or heard five species of summer migrants, and found a chalice-shaped hole in the riverbed that contained the uncorrupted bodies of a wheatear and a stonechat.

* * *

So that was the season of light. Stooping always over it, like a schoolmaster trying to catch me out in an act of enjoyment, was the season of darkness.

I can no longer pretend that the winter is fine. I have tried to tell myself that the country is not dead, but resting and regrouping, stroking the inchoate life inside it, and that that's what is happening to me, too. But it won't do anymore. Although it's biological nonsense, the land is dead to me. I can't feel any solidarity with it. It's dead, and I'm not: I wouldn't panic as I do if I were. I resent the land for being dead. I've kept faith with it, and this is the way it treats me. It goes and dies, just when it's needed. It will come back, but that's resurrection, not resuscitation. I don't need salvation eventually: I need it now. There's no slow heartbeat to hear when I lie with my ear to the ground in a January wood. The mist curling up from the combe isn't the slow breath of cold trees; it's the stenchless stench of a long-dead corpse.

There's a sort of winter life, I know. Waders and waterfowl come to the shore; there are redwings and fieldfares on the common. But these are like maggots feeding on the carcass of the year; their movement is horrible. I sit by the fire with cider and a book, getting fat and cold and bitter. I endure, and mark off the days on the cell wall.

This is not a good attitude for someone writing a book about the natural world. I'm supposed to feign a cheerful fascination with all the faces of the land; to talk merrily about the joys of storm and frost and woolly socks. I can't do it. This is an incomplete writer, and an incomplete book. The otters stay when the sun goes, but I'm hardly there with them.

I've tried to stay; I really have. But I've just been going through the motions. Sometimes the motions have been fairly strenuous. I've floated and stumbled in December down from Badgworthy to Watersmeet—stumbling because the proprioceptors in my limbs stopped telling me where those limbs were in space. I've rummaged in January in the flooded roots of the waterside trees, expecting big sluggish fish to be dozing there, but getting nothing but fingers like blue carrots. And, knowing that the cold, and that urgent calorific imperative, sends otters wandering ever more widely, I've tramped and tramped the riverbanks and the watersheds, trying to feel in touch with them—or in touch with anything outside myself. I've failed. It's like sitting in the Bodleian Library, besieged by email, my brain bruised to spasm and uselessness by the attrition of all the daily littlenesses. The cold of the moor does that to me, too. The littlenesses have to stop before my brain can come out of spasm and grasp things again. The sun has to come back before there's any chance of empathy, or even half-decent observation, on the riverbank. But when it does! When it does, there's the euphoric *whoo-whoop* of the depressive surging back onto a manic wave top. Then I'm not just a pedestrian sniffer of spraint and a trudging, grudging collector of adjectives: I'm a bloomin', blooming shaman, impossible to live with, pretentious beyond endurance.

But I can't do the winter. You should ask for 25 percent off the price of this book.

This tells me something worth knowing. A depressed shaman, hunter, or naturalist can't work at all. A gray soul, apparently, can't penetrate that thin veil between the species.

I don't understand the metaphysics. But it seems that you have to be sufficiently *I* to be another, and depression erodes the *I* below the critical point. Perhaps, for a human, being an animal is just an extreme mode of empathy—no different in kind from what you need to be a decent lover or father or colleague. When you're depressed, you might simply be nursing that injured *I* too obsessively to have the energy or attention necessary for empathy. Our nursing strategies are radically misconceived. They all tend to be based on the disastrous misconception that if you give your self away there will be less of you. In fact, of course (as we know when the sun shines), the very opposite is true.

Or perhaps you prefer the epic language of the shaman. Travel between worlds is a strenuous business, not for those with any disability. Remember the Levitical prohibition on disabled priests? And the shamanic world is a gift culture: the gift required is the only one you can give—yourself. The spirit otters guarding the gate won't beckon you in with welcoming paws to a sumptuous eel feast if they see you limping or bearing, wrapped in lily leaves and red ribbon, a mere effigy of yourself. They demand the real thing.

* * *

I'd served my apprenticeship and made my maps during the day. But the night was the real business. I'd put it off and off. It's one thing to romp through moonlit bracken being a badger: that's like being an excited Cub Scout on his first camp. It's quite another to lie on the bottom of a pool at midnight with ancient things cruising around. That's like being dead. I needed to be pushed into the river, or lured by the prospect of sensual excitement. The river was kind. I was lured.

I left the Staghunters' Inn after a night of pool and a few

pints of beer and plunged straight into dark diluted only by starlight.

The Staghunters' is a gentle, murmuring place. It clicks, clinks, and giggles. By the time I pulled on my (new) jacket, said good-bye, and stepped out onto the rippling ribbon of river sound that runs along the road, my ears had changed: they'd started off small and applied conventionally to the side of my head. Fifty yards down the road they were the size of cabbages, and had started to swivel. Another fifty yards, and they'd dropped into my ankles, and I heard voles better than I heard owls. Yet another fifty, and they'd multiplied, and sprouted from my front and sides like bracket fungi. It was fifteen more minutes, while I was climbing through the wood to the ridge, before my retinas accommodated and gave me badger eyes. *If I jumped naked into the river*, I suddenly thought, *I'd have the eyes in two, and the river would throw in a whole stack of new ears, too.*

So the next night I walked over the bridge and along the path (dodging, by memory, the piles of dog shit), stripped by an ash tree, stood on a rock like an overnourished sacrifice to a jealous Aegean god, and jumped in among the cock salmon. When my head broke back up through the film of foam and mayflies I had a thick, leprous skin of seamless ears like the compound eyes of a bluebottle, each of them sucking in sound. This, to begin with, was far too much sensation for sense. My brain knew what to do with sound beamed into the sides of my head. It couldn't cope with sound from my little toe and my shoulder. It got dizzy with overload and with the unaccustomed angles, and complained, queasily, just as your stomach and your semicircular canals complain when you're being centrifuged, along with the cotton candy, at a fairground. But then my brain pulled up its neuronal socks, realized that it was up to the job of coordinating the broadcasts from each of its distant, outlandish outstations, and swelled proprietorially, announcing that its body was big and young and capable of doing new, strange stuff. "Have you never heard with your knee?" it said. "Ha! Call yourself a human?"

Sound travels more than four times faster in water than in air. When you're down in the water, relying mainly on sound and feeling rather than sight, distances are exhilaratingly shrunk. A crayfish clattering across gravel fifty yards away sounds as if it's at the end of your arm. The water filling your ears is a megaphone. If your only sense is phonic, things swell. Those clacking claws are monstrous. They'd usually occur only in lurid Jurassic dreams. The nighttime pool is epic, a legendary playground.

Anyone who has paid good money to lie in a flotation tank (why would anyone do that, when there are rivers?) knows what happens when you turn down the dimmer switch on one set of senses. All the others are switched more fully on. (To switch them actually *fully* on is a yogic enterprise.)

I used a flashlight that first night in the river. I never used it again. Flashlights are an abomination. They don't illuminate: they obscure. They drain the night of its color, and freeze fluid animals. The rods in our retinas, which work at low light intensities, create black-and-white pictures; but whether by some immense subtlety of the retina itself, or by some cunning central processing, the grays of night are as varied as the rainbow spectrum of noon. It's not just that we translate a particular combination of grays into the combination of colors that we know it represents. The neuro-alchemy is more mysterious than that. Our night brains aren't just pretending, pathetically but convincingly, that it's day. There's a wholesale translation of our brain into the brain of a night thing—one of the most complete and joyful shape-shiftings we can know. Like all graces, it is a fragile thing, and our instinct is to smash it up. This is easily done. A flick of the switch, and you're back in a world that doesn't exist at all, either in the day or in the night: you're a creature of lithium-cadmium. We have a depraved craving for not-places, for not-food, for not-people. And so we buy flashlights.

Humans, made bionic by a cold bath, can see, hear, and (before the cold knocks out their peripheral sensation) feel the most wonderful night things in the river. The river day is frigid. The weed waves prettily enough, but like sterile surgical drapes, with no erotic promise. It might as well be wallpaper, or an overcurated exhibit in a clinically lighted, centrally heated museum. But at night it grabs your legs and strokes them up to the crotch. Sunlight rinses color from the weed: lubricious blacks, reds, and browns slink back when the sun's gone. In the dark wood the night clots; in the river the night is in solution.

That first river night spoiled the river days for me. But even the night couldn't redeem the winter.

* * *

In my first summer on the East Lyn River I'd found a place where the water races through a tight spout into a deep pool. It travels so fast that it's pushed right to the bottom of the pool, carrying with it the air it has collected in the stony avenue that runs down from the moor—air full of greenness and birdsong. It hits the rock at the foot of the pool and spirals back, right to the top, weaving around the downward bubbles in an incomprehensible double helix. That first day, I put my face in it and made myself a mask of air with streamers down my head like silver dreadlocks. When my face was in it, I had a million compound eyes, like an enormous fly. They smashed up the light and shot it into my retinas with a violence that made ordinary vision old and tired. I molded the bubbles the way a potter molds clay on the wheel—pushing the helix in to make a waist, and pulling it out in strands. In the light-

seasons I went religiously to the spout once a week. It became a sabbath.

Otters, too, take time out from the mania. They play with the water—pointlessly, if the only possible point is the acquisition of calories and the maximizing of reproductive potential. But only when the spring comes and the input-output equations look healthier. Same for me.

When the spring gave me back to myself (how amazing to be able to use the words—*spring* and *myself*—for the first time since October), I came up out of the earth, an elated escapee from the dark camp behind me, and slipped back epiphanically into the water.

"You'll feel the change in your face," growled a Scottish farmer I knew. He was talking about the weather, or puberty, or sheep dip poisoning, or orgasm. But it's not a bad general observation about the world. I felt the change in my face. It didn't grin, but it had possibilities again.

Otters experience the world mainly through the change in their faces. Their faces are chisels thrusting between the layers of river water. They're the first bit of the animal to cross the sudden seam between the shallow-warmed water above Rockford and the old, cold, green water sludging up from the dark basins. All that is obvious. But the intensity of the sensation is not.

Above my desk is the mask of a big otter killed by hounds somewhere in Dorset in the 1930s. He looks defiantly martial, as he no doubt was when his final attempt to escape the stockade of thundering poles failed and he turned at last to try to rip the testicles off the booming lead hound.

Part of that martial look, I've realized, is his whiskers. They're Prussian in their belligerence. They're the whiskers of treaty and border violation; of smoking cannon and multiple amputations. In other words, they are long, thick, stiff.

They are buried deep in the skin of his face. In life the base of each whisker lay in a densely woven nest of sensory receptors. From each nest, thick nerve cables coursed away toward that febrile brain, which collated the information and translated it into a picture of the world. Was it a visual picture? Was the end product something like "Fishy and edible three feet to the north-northwest," and marked by an image of a fish, generated by a buzz in the visual cortex and flashed around to the paws, the teeth, and the appetite? I suspect so. Otters are insufficiently olfactory or auditory for any other type of stamp to be likely, and surely *some* stamp is inevitable. In normal circumstances we translate to visual: the scent of a fire or a woman becomes an image; a musical cadence conjures the sight of a landscape or of the concert hall where we first heard it. Only in extreme circumstances—and notably during sex—does the translation stop, and we experience touch or smell or sound as it is—qua caress, musk, or gasp. We're closest to a hunting otter when we're in a bed with a lover.

The knowledge of death first trembled deep inside the cheeks of my Prussian otter. As it lay in the river, all but its nostrils submerged, it would have heard first the chatter about scent and rural adultery and the hunt ball and the inadequacy of the cakes and then, more ominously, a hound speaking from the wood under the alders, and others joining it in a rolling chorus of menace. It may have got a whiff of vol-au-vents and macassar oil and the sour urine and dead-calf belch of excited dogs. But none of this mattered much: it had all happened before. Not until the pressure waves from the thrashing legs of hounds bounced off the kingfisher tree and shivered through the water to those whiskers did things get serious. Even then it was a time for cunning and not for fear. Only when the cheeks thrilled to the water rushing direct and hard from hounds' legs churning like millwheels was it time to dart and turn rather than cruise; and only when the cheeks were over-whelmed, and gave way to sight, was it the end.

Although the nerve cables and the distant processing are important, the local sensation in the cheeks must remain intense. The otter's head must be like a perpetually engorged glans, pushing desperately into the world, seeking always more sensation.

There wasn't much I could do to reeducate my cheeks. Certainly growing whiskers myself didn't work. My whiskers made my face less sensate, not more. They weren't buried in a fizzing mass of nerve endings, and, being flaccid things, didn't move much with wind or water or touch, and so didn't transmit much to their pathetic complement of nerves. I was far better off shaving as close as I could before jumping into a river, and avoiding like the plague those anesthetic alcohol-based aftershaves that would probably kill all wildlife, like sheep dip.

Yet I can understand what it's like to be cheek-o-centric. It's far more intimate to reach out and touch another's cheek than to reach down and touch their genitals. A kiss is correspondingly more erotic than sexual intercourse. Everyone knows that prostitutes won't kiss: there are some things that aren't ever for sale.

I tried to push into the world more consciously with my face. I bent my head forward when I came into a room. I tried not to advance toward new people with my hand extended (as I'd been told from birth was how gentlemen behaved) or swaggeringly foot-first (as it had been insinuated at public school was the way to make your mark, showing that you're a man with legs to march across other people's countries and feet to kick the butts of the workers).

I lingered longer in the sexless cheek-to-cheek greetings of the middle class, getting known as a deviant. I nuzzled lawns, chairs, door frames, cake, tablecloths, trees, and trains.

I lay long in rivers, facing the current, telling myself to notice the shape of the water-storms and leas made by the crown of my head, and the fussier, angrier ones made by my nose. A horse leech fastened to my lip, and I didn't notice for an hour.

It was all rather silly. Cold water quickly makes the face as numb as a pork knuckle, and although I could channel a bit more of my mind into my face, I couldn't make my face behave like fingertips—even like the fingertips of my own hands, mutilated as they are by Arctic frostbite and Scottish rock fall.

But I could, I slowly realized, turn my fingertips into whiskers. Any decent somatotopic map would have told me that that was a sensible thing to do. That, in fact, would emulate the otters' neural world quite well. I couldn't teach my fingers to decode, as I imagine an otter's vibrissae do, the pressure contours of the river. But generally those whiskers aren't acting alone, like a single antenna on a high ridge: they're acting in busy, bloody concert with the teeth and the front paws.

* * *

We've all seen exciting underwater sequences in which, with symphonic elegance and grandeur, otters chase huge fish in huge tanks, just as cheetahs hunt antelope in the Serengeti (and often with the same soundtrack), weaving and turning with such speed that they're clearly moving through the virtual space between the water molecules rather than through the water itself. The show ends with the triumphant otter in the shallows, struggling to shift the dead fish and taking a bite out of where the fish's shoulder would be if fish had shoulders.

Forget it. At least for most English otters most of the time. I've only rarely found big fish bones in the spraints of Devon otters. Our hard-pressed otters are often pushed to options two and three in their spreadsheet. They are bottom feeders: they turn over stones with their front paws and hope for a panicky bullhead to bolt past their whiskers. As the Somerset otter man James Williams observed, it's like nothing so much as cricket: the little fish come off the bat at an angle, and the slip-fielding otters dive for the catch. There's not much meat on a bullhead, but there are a lot of them, they're there throughout the year, and a bit of gentle fielding isn't anything like as energy consuming as those Tchaikovskian pursuits of big game.

Otters, then, are highly tactile fumblers. It's quite effective fumbling. In the fumbling, but not the efficacy, I can follow them. Like everyone, I've tried chasing big fish, and like everyone who's not armed with a spear gun I've failed (though once, wearing fins in a sea pool on Kintyre, I touched the tail of a sea trout and thought I was a god).

I fumbled particularly in the Badgworthy. It's easiest in fairly shallow water, where you can lie face-first, breathing through a snorkel. Often I used just a snorkel, with no mask, hoping that my face and my fingers would be more alive. And then, more or less blindly, I turned over stones with my nose or my hands. When I used my nose, I made a net around the stone by cradling it with my arms. When I used a hand, I pushed my head right up to the stone to block one plane of escape, and tried to cover the other routes by circling them with my other arm.

It wasn't a great success: I managed to grab a couple of blotchy stone loaches and a truculent miller's-thumb. A disoriented stickleback, no doubt taking my open mouth for a cave, swam inside. Its fluttering spines grazed my palate like the probe of a Parkinsonian dentist. I should have crushed it between my fillings and swallowed it. I couldn't, any more than I could stamp on a mouse. My failure is illogical: I pay good money for other people to winch cows bellowing to their deaths so that we can serve up buttock muscle for Sunday lunch. My illogicality isn't original, of course, which perhaps makes it worse, and certainly makes it less interesting. It's about distance; about vicarious guilt being less intense; about the little physiological details of death that speak more intimately to our moral intuitions than any amount of argument; about the fact that physical proximity connotes relationship, even with a very basic animal, and that almost any sort of relationship makes it harder to kill.

I killed a fish with my teeth once, as a very young child, and by accident. I was by a pond in Yorkshire, with a jam jar full of small darting things, including a minnow.

"Put it in your mouth," said Chris. "I dare you."

And I did. Not only that, but I pretended to chew it. Then, in an early and dramatic illustration of the terrible principle that you tend to become what you pretend to be, I chopped it by mistake. Its muddy guts, full of midge larvae and aquatic worms, spilled over my tongue. The flapping electricity of its death quivered into my gums. I spat it into the pond. It was still twitching as a shoal of other minnows rose to eat it.

"Cool," said Chris, horrified.

"That was good," said I, far more horrified.

* * *

I didn't enjoy turning over stones. This was mainly due to my phobia of lampreys. This phobia is yet another reason why I'm not qualified to write this chapter. For otters love them.

The phobia is biologically unintelligent. The Badgworthy Water has mostly brook lampreys, which don't parasitize other fish, and river lampreys, which are much less common there, and have better things to do than try to burrow in through the thick hide of a large mammal. Yet I couldn't shake the picture out of my head: the sucker and those rasping jaws that eat into the side and then in, in, in, through the internal organs, until the host dies. Then the fat lamprey squeezy-squirms out between the ribs and goes off to spawn or to search for another animal.

Vedius Pollio planned to kill one of his slaves, who'd broken a cup, by throwing him into a pool of lampreys. The slave screamed (I can hear the screams now) and begged to be killed in any other way. The Emperor Augustus, who was staying at the villa, was appalled, canceled the decree, and ordered that all of Pollio's remaining cups be smashed. Quite right.

That's the sort of thing that was with me at the bottom of the Badgworthy Water.

Lampreys are a serious argument against the goodness or omnipotence of God. And so it might be argued that anything that kills them with enthusiasm is an agent of light. That thought's the closest I've come to feeling warm about otters.

* * *

By and large our relationships with fish are emotionally uncomplicated. No child really loves its goldfish. The magnate who shells out big money for koi carp loves the price tag, or the status, or the associated engineering, or the mere idea, or, in his better moments, the lugubrious rolling and stirring—the pace of the fish. But never the fish itself. When a desperate otter breaks in and pulls out the koi pool's emperor by its gilded face, the children won't sentimentally stroke or ceremonially inter the fish remains. A man who wouldn't dream of accelerating his BMW over a rabbit will happily winch mackerel into the air (a journey for them as far, and as significant, as being blasted to Jupiter would be for a human) and beam for the camera as they flappingly suffocate on the deck. The same man might well, without a wince, put hooks into the body of a live fish and let it thrash paroxysmally away in the hope of getting a bigger fish to swallow it. As a species we have a congenital, curious, and nearly complete lack of imagination and empathy when it comes to fish.

But with crustaceans it's more complex. Yes, we boil them

alive and stick spikes in their heads, but we often issue little murmurs of apology as we do. This is very strange: they are at least as different from us (and therefore as blithely killable) as fish. Evolutionary eons stand between them and our empathy. You'd have thought that the separation would be made more complete by that armored chitinous coat.

I think it's to do with the eyes. Crustacean eyes don't wink, or have lashes or brows or expressions, but they're out there: they protrude; they come toward us; they wave to us. Or perhaps it's those arms, raised and opened to us in aggression that looks like welcome. We can't help thinking that they're making overtures to us. We can't entirely resist the suggestion of relationship. Perhaps we only ever respond to what is like us. Fish eyes are flat. Ours aren't. We think that flat things can't have souls. And since fish don't have arms, and so can't hug, we assume that they don't want to be hugged.

Whatever: otters don't care. They need the calories. We are not like them: we often empathize when it's really costly, although we're depressingly good at choking down our empathy.

There are lots of crayfish in the river that runs by our Oxford house, and in the stream in the wood where the children run wild. The children brought a big one back in a plastic bag and put it on my face as I lay on the kitchen floor.

I'd thought that big crayfish would make an otter cautious—that those claws would engender a bit of respect. But this big crayfish was a tentative, almost gentle thing. Yes, it stabbed at my closed eyes when I poked at it, took hold of my nose and swung off my nostrils when I moved, and raised and stretched itself in that belligerent patriarchal welcome. But it was all rather pathetic. All the elaborate armoring and posturing wouldn't even be like a whisper of breeze on the face of that otter, powering out of the dark and flattening the cray-fish against the stones with a commanding paw.

We put it in the freezer to kill it, and the boys fried it with chili oil.

* * *

Just as I'd put off the night river, I'd put off the sea. Both were like death. I am neither old enough nor young enough to write about the sea. It is both too big to be described and too basic to need description.

The land was like me: secondary, derivative, the product of comprehensible forces. The sea was not like me. Yet I wondered if I'd get closest to otters there, because the sea is strange even to most otters. It was hard to follow otters when they were being themselves in the East Lyn, but that was mostly because their true selves were so elusive. If we met in a place where we were both alien, we might understand each other better, as embattled refugees from different war zones have an uneasy fellowship. But whether or not that was right, the sea couldn't be put off indefinitely.

I floated and scrambled to the sea from Watersmeet, where the river writhes with trout, fat. At night I could have stalked the fish with the flashlight I've so piously denounced. In the day I couldn't help snapping at them like a puppy. An otter wouldn't have bothered. If it had gotten this far downstream it would have hurried on, knowing that there were shoals of scaly succulence just beyond the smack and suck of the surf.

There are huge tides here in the Bristol Channel, but the land is so steep that you don't feel them. They keep to the sea. There's land here, and there's sea here, but little no-man's-land. For a few hours each day there's a soapy, brackish ambiguity for a couple of hundred yards at Lynmouth, but the invaded land doesn't stop being land, just as the water stoats that we call otters don't stop being stoats.

Yet there's a scouring and a scraping and a screeching of stones and birds that roll through the water. In the dead of night, which is the life of night, the otters swim past the pasty shops into a forest of kelp and gut weed, just as I floated down like an inner tube one bright March morning. The fish there are a new kind of moon-silver. The crabs cracked (it would have sounded like crackling wireless in an old submarine) by an otter at the harbor mouth are descended from crabs that ate children who drifted out on their air mattresses, fishermen who stayed too long for one more box of fish, and dead otters washed down from the moor. And I can join with them; we can all eat each other.

The sea is different. It's not just land water and rock crumble. The land and the sea have different rulers, and so different rules. The moon tugs all the time at everything in the sea. The land is insulated from the moon. At most, the moon cuts on a clear night a few feet into river and lake water. There's a moon tide inside the bodies of earth women, but that's because they're all mermaids. ("Yeah, right," said Burt.) You see land fish wallowing in moonlight, but that's because it's a luxurious novelty. It's like bubble bath for them. In the sea there's no escape from the moon. You can't have a moonless swim any more than a saltless swim.

Land otters, when they come to the sea, are at sea—as tentative and as baffled as I am. They lollop along the long bleak beach at Dunster, at the edge of the surf, like little children; for all the world as if they're frightened of getting their feet wet, but with a vacationer's delight in the fear.

* * *

"This is fun," said an otter-child who'd been swept down the East Lyn and then out to sea with me. "At least for a while." I wasn't so sure, because by then I was more of an otter than he was.

4. Fox

The Tube is a syringe, pushing a solution of bodies and electric air into the city's limbs.

When you ooze out of Bethnal Green station, there's a grimy brick building by the road with a tired sign: COME UNTO ME AND I WILL GIVE YOU REST.

There's a café around the corner. It used to be run by gentle, stammering, self-effacing Buddhists, and I used to regroup there over cheese and onion rolls after romantic routs. Now it's full of shrill, carefully unshaven metrosexuals eating pine nuts. There's a metallic noise that is either music or bad plumbing. Everyone's thin, and no one's enjoying being thin.

Outside that café, squeezed at both ends into calligraphic flourishes, was my first London fox scat, coruscating with purple beetles.

When I first came here it was a less brash, more confident place. People lived here because they did, rather than because they should. There was no corrosive apartheid between the drinkers of *ristretto* and the eaters of pie and mash.

Back then I would read a book and eat penne arrabbiata

most nights down Globe Road, drain a carafe of rough Chianti, and take a loop of the park before heading home. One warm October night, steering between drug dealers and copulating couples, I saw two foxes on the grass by the bandstand. They swung their heads smoothly over the ground like placid vacuum cleaners, each swing marking a silver furrow in the dew. I crept closer. They took no notice. I crept very close: they raised their heads, saw that I wasn't a dog or a car, and went back to their swinging. They were harvesting crane flies. The ground was thick with them. The crane flies were laying eggs. That takes time, and anyway, the damp stuck their wings to the grass like stamps in an album. The foxes just had to peel them off with their tongues and suck them up.

I got down on my knees beside the foxes and grazed. There seemed nothing barbarous about crushing bodies that were so slight, so dry, and so still. A victim needs to have viscera to evoke visceral disgust. The crane flies were pinioned by the surface tension and didn't move much. Think of a ticklish rice paper garnish that turns to vanilla slime.

Half an hour later the foxes were still there, systematically working their patch under the sodium lighting, as I got stiffly up and walked home in a ruined suit.

It wasn't the first time I had tried to be a fox. When I was nine my father arrived home, excited: "Look what's in the back of the car. But be very careful."

There, in black plastic trash bags, were two recently dead foxes—a dog and a vixen. Their lips were pulled back in a snarl. They looked angry to be dead. The vixen had swollen mammary glands. She had obviously been suckling cubs.

"Don't touch their teeth," said my father. "They've been killed with strychnine."

That's not a nice way to die. A farmer had once delightedly told me what it did to moles, and I could understand the bitterness of that fixed smile. Very soon after taking the poison, probably planted on a dead lamb, these foxes would have felt tremors and rising nausea. The tremors would have towered up, powered up, and turned into convulsions. In a dark field in Derbyshire they'd have repeatedly arched and extended their backs almost until they snapped, and then, when their diaphragms finally gave out, they'd have turned blue and died in an asphyxial froth of blood and foam. They were achingly lovely. From then on I signed off all my letters with the head of a fox.

We went out to try to find the cubs. We lay for three nights under a tarpaulin downwind of a hole in a hill. I bought a chicken with my birthday money, disemboweled and dismembered it, and spread it tantalizingly around near the entrance to the hole.

This was a time when I thought I could will anything. I willed the cubs to come out. I asked (not knowing whom or what I was asking) to be possessed by those adult foxes so that I could know where the cubs were, or persuade them that it was safe to emerge.

We shivered and we willed. They never came. It was my first real disillusionment.

If I'd been in Japan, the fox spirits would have jumped at my invitation. There they don't need to be asked in at all, let alone asked twice. Plenty of people in Japan are married, often unknowingly, and often satisfactorily, to eyelash-batting, stiletto-wearing fox spirits. It's not always good, though, and fox exorcism is big business. In everyday life you've got to be careful that you're not being beguiled by a fox. The danger's greatest over the phone, when you can't see the person you're talking to (presumably Skype is making it tougher for spirit-foxes), and telephonic conventions have developed to avert it. There are some human sounds that foxes can't pronounce, such as *moshi moshi*. They're part of the standard greeting. If your opposite number doesn't use it, hang up.

But these Derbyshire foxes evidently took their metaphysics, like their rabbits, from the land, and the High Peak is part of the West. Here, foxes are the definitive other: they won't cross the species boundary except when, as demonic agents, they tunnel into the soul, making it foul with their stench, and mixing their dung with the mess of bloody feathers from other plundered souls.

Foxes let in disillusionment. They also let in death. The house, my bedroom, and the shed to which I and my skins and bottles of formalin had been banished were full of corpses. But I hadn't really identified the corpses as dead. They were just little peninsulas of wilderness that reached gloriously behind our pebble-dashed walls; aids to *living* fully, unlike the people all around us in suburbia; nothing to do with extinction. They were silent and still, but that just meant it was easier to study them than if they'd been slinking or flapping. It didn't mean that they had stopped being, or that they represented a threat to me or to anyone I cared about.

That changed when I was eleven. Here is the entry in my nature diary:

February 2

Found dead fox (*Vulpes vulpes crucigera*) down on a large patch of grass in the Mayfield valley. It was in a bad state of decomposition and Rigor Mortis seemed fully developed in the limbs.* Strangely enough, this specimen had been very neatly skinned. The skull and everything else on the carcass was intact. There were many maggots on the carcass which were all dead, probably because of the cold night. We took from the body the skull (including the lower jaws and teeth) and the bones of the tail. We took these home and boiled

---

* I was plainly wrong about the rigor mortis. The dead maggots indicated that the rigor mortis must have passed long before.

them to clean the unwanted matter off. We then bleached
them in household bleach (chlorous).

A sketch map followed.

The prose is revealingly constipated. There's plainly something missing. What's missing is the soul-rattling shock I
felt. This fox was dead in a way that the strychnine foxes had
not been, and for a fox to be dead was really pretty serious.
Apart from swifts, foxes were the most obviously alive things
I knew. I'd watched them alongside lean, wired, taut dogs.
Even when the dogs were racing hard, the foxes sauntered. The
very best dogs slouch; foxes glide. If even foxes could be killed
this emphatically, nothing was safe: not my parents, not my
sister, and not me. The grave opened.

And then, as I was still standing there in that cold field,
came another thought: this very, very dead fox is more alive
than a correspondingly dead dog. So an ontological snobbery
was born: a belief in a hierarchy of being. Some being was so
mighty that it would survive even cardiac arrest. It made me
an insufferable little shit for years. I've never recovered, and
nor have several of the people who've had to put up with me.

But here's the relevance for this book: I felt that if I wanted
to be like a fox I could do it by, first of all, being very alive
(which was a comfort) or by being splendidly dead (which is
a rather stranger comfort).

* * *

Foxes trickled up with the Pleistocene ice, then trickled down
railway lines and canal fringes into the inner cities. They are
Tories. Urban fox numbers correlate perfectly with blue
rosettes. They like the gardens that come with affluence. Some
commute—in both directions. Many (though not my East End
foxes) have nice, leafy country houses, and come to town, like
the men in suits, for the rich, easy pickings of the city. Others

choose to live and raise cubs under a lawyer's shed by the Tube station, and to relax and get a breath of fresh air in the country.

The East End of London doesn't vote Tory, despite the corporate laptops and the mango *jus,* and the foxes here are hard-pressed. There are shed-owning lawyers whose kids like to feed foxes, but they're in small ghettos with polished floorboards, walled in by towering concrete cabinets where the desperate are filed.

The humans here have small brains. Smaller, that is, than the wild men from whom they descended. They've shrunk about 10 percent over the last ten thousand years. Since dogs faithfully follow their masters, their brains have shrunk too. Dog brains are about 25 percent smaller than those of wolves—their immediate ancestor. Domestication makes everything shrivel.

We don't know what effect inner-city living will have on foxes, but urban foxes have lost no length or weight. It's not surprising. Even in the fat suburbs, where they could live off bird tables, hedgehog food, and the interested benevolence of the middle class, they choose to hunt. Like us, they are built to be multivalent. It's how they and we triumphed over heat, ice, drought, and monoculturalists. Strenuous though it is for them—demanding a lot more ingenuity and energy than it takes simply to pick up pizza and lap up sweet-and-sour sauce—they've opted to listen, pounce, prospect, and innovate. We haven't. In a few generations we've turned into sclerosed superspecialists, each in a niche so tight that our limbs can't stretch and our brains can't turn. I bet foxes' choices will keep their brains throbbingly big and keen and their legs like steel wire when we can't hoist ourselves from the sofa.

* * *

It's easy enough to march to the urban fox's beat. They are those most onomatopoeic of creatures: crepuscular. They live, by preference, and as befits brilliant physiological generalists, along the mucky tideline where the night washes into the day. Here in the East End, though, there are no proper nights: just dirty days and nights of scorching twilight. For these foxes, the dusk is not the dimming of the light, but the thinning of the traffic. Sound and tremble take over from photons. When the taxis have dropped off most of the bankers, out come the foxes. They forage over a big area here (probably getting on for half a square mile) and show the generic fox's caching behavior. They forage or hunt, then cache (usually burying, in an often rather messy, approximate way), and then continue to forage and hunt and cache before returning to cached food. It's hard to bury under asphalt: my foxes shove food clumsily under pallets and cardboard boxes used to deliver wide-screen TVs. Then, the territory trawled, they select what they need (going for the most toothsome first) and head home.

The traffic-dawn and the sun-dawn more or less coincide. Trucks shudder down the Old Ford Road; Porsches purr off to Canary Wharf; buses rumble west to disgorge people into open-plan, air-conditioned slavery, with cooled water dispensers. The foxes lick last night's *aloo gobi* off their lips and curl up under the shed.

* * *

The more respectably dressed you are, the harder it is to be a fox. No one has ever accused me of being respectably dressed, but even so, I soon realized that I should be even more shabbily shambolic than usual. Someone in unstained trousers and an unripped sweater looks criminal if he's raking through a herniated bin bag, but if you're dirty, tired, and slumped, no one minds. You're translucent. People look through you. The grubbier you are, the more translucent you are. If you're on all fours, sniffing at a sack, you're invisible. Except to the authorities. And even there, sleeping is more offensive than doing.

I was shaken awake under the rhododendrons.

"Afternoon, sir."

"Good afternoon."

"Can I help at all, sir?"

"No thanks. All's fine."

"Can I ask what you're doing, sir?"

"Just having a little sleep, officer."

"I'm afraid you can't sleep here, sir. You sure you're okay, sir?"

"Fine, thank you. And what's the problem with sleeping here?"

"It's forbidden, as I'm sure you know. Trespassing. The owners can't have people just sleeping."

(Just sleeping?)

"I can't see that I'm interfering materially with the enjoyment of its title of a property management company registered in Panama."

"Are you trying to be clever, sir?"

I could think of no palatable answer to this. The policeman didn't press me for one. He moved to another topic.

"Why do you have to sleep here, may I ask?"

"You may indeed ask, but I don't suppose you'll like the answer. I'm trying to be a fox, and" (I rushed on, trying to avert my eyes from the torrential hemorrhage of the officer's residual goodwill) "I want to know what it's like to listen all day to traffic and to look at ankles and calves rather than at whole people."

This last observation was a bad, bad mistake. I knew it as soon as it was out. For him, calves, ankles, and concealment in an evergreen shrub meant perversion so deep that it should be measured in years inside. But I could see him struggling to identify the right pigeonhole for my depravity, and imagining the paperwork. Uncertainty and workload trumped his instincts, and he told me to "bugger off home, *sir*" (the italics were powerful on his lips) "and get a life."

"That," I said, "is exactly what I'm trying to get."

He looked paternalistically at me as I brushed the leaves off my jersey and walked home.

After that I cravenly slept under a tarp in my backyard.

* * *

Foxes sometimes sleep on the median strip of freeways. Three thousand vehicles an hour shriek past in oily vortices of dust, rubber, deodorant, vomit, electric muttering, and what we've absurdly come to call power. I've slept on the shoulder of a highway myself, beneath a canopy of cow parsley and dock, wanting to be violated by noise and palpitation, and still being shocked by the un-brute brutality of the thrusting pistons. Even the most wanton wrenchings of the natural world—wild dogs in a tug-of-war with a baby gazelle, for instance—are tender and proper beside the violence of a bus or a train.

A fox can hear a squeaking vole a hundred yards away, and rooks winging across fields a third of a mile off. To lie ten yards from a speeding van must be apocalyptic: like living inside a tornado. Even the sneezing, snoring, grumbling, humming, moaning, turning, deep night of the inner city is a cacophonous fairground.

It's the fox's plasticity that so daunts me. I can get an intellectual, or at least a poetical, grip on acute sensitivity in another animal. But acute sensitivity *and* intense toleration: that's hard. And it's not as if it is mere reluctant toleration for the sake of survival, like the badgers who, because suitable habitats are hard to find, might put up with a rather suboptimal railway embankment. Foxes seem to *enjoy* being outrageous. They flaunt their thriving in conditions that are objectively wretched. They don't want my loud, tree-hugging sermons on their behalf, and I feel not only miffed but mystified. They are the true citizens of the world. I'm not, and I rather resent them for bettering me. I also don't understand how they do it, either physiologically or emotionally.

You'd expect a truly cosmopolitan creature to make some costly compromises, to give up some hearing in return for better eyes, or some smell for some sight. Surely generalists can't be great specialists? But they are. I'm in awe.

* * *

I hated the East End. It's an offense. It was built on marshland as a refugee camp, and it is now a workhouse from which, because of poverty or wealth, few can afford to escape. Few would say, these days, that it's home, and even fewer would say so gladly. Few people really live here at all. They beam their thoughts in from outer space; they fly their food in from Thailand and their fripperies from China; their furniture sails in a steel box from Sweden. I suppose that's not really so far. We are, after all, made of stardust.

Though foxes are made of stardust, too, and eat Thai chicken curry, they're genuinely local. They know the taste of every square inch of concrete; they've looked from a range of about three inches at every spreading stain of lichen up to eighteen inches from the ground; they know that there's a mouse nest under the porch at number 17A and bumblebees by the cedar decking at number 29B. They've watched the tedious adulteries of Mrs. S, Mr. K being carted off to die, and the psychosis of the M twins blossoming from petty backyard cruelties into much worse. They know the flight paths of jumbo jets and greylag geese. Under the shed they nestle among the oysters that gave the local Victorians typhoid. They walk around the area for nearly five miles a night, and they do it with everything switched on.

But they're not around for long. Being an urban fox is an intense, dangerous business. Sixty percent of London's foxes die each year. Eighty-eight percent of Oxford foxes die before their second birthday. They know bereavement. There's only a 16 percent chance that both animals of a fox pair that have raised cubs in their first reproductive year will survive for a second breeding season. They don't just know the fact of bereavement; they feel it—apparently as I do, and make similar sounds.

David Macdonald, who has conducted, from his base in Oxford, much of the most significant work on fox behavior, kept pet foxes. (He commented that his landlady found his flat curiously hard to rent when he left it. Not everyone shares my, or his, taste for the smell of fox urine.) One of his vixens was caught in the flailing blades of a grass cutter. A leg dangled by a thread of tissue. Macdonald's distraught wife picked her up. The vixen's mate tried to pull the vixen away as she was carried to the car, and he looked after the car as it drove down the path.

The next day the vixen's sister picked up a mouthful of food at a cache and ran off with it, whimpering as foxes do when they're giving food to cubs. She hadn't called like that for over a year. She took the food to the grass hollow where, the night before, her sister had bled. She buried it beneath the blood-stained blades of grass.

This has the pathos of my own story, and it was this that made me more anthropomorphic about foxes than about any of my other animals. I felt more confident about reading them right than about the others.

* * *

Foxes and dogs are very, very different. They're in different genera. They parted company about 12 million years ago—a divergence reflected in the number of chromosomes: domestic dogs (evolved wolves) have 78 pairs; red foxes 34 to 38 pairs. You needn't put your poodle on the pill if there's a libidinous dog fox oiling around. And yet there's *something* to be learned about foxes from looking at dogs.

Dogs are specialists in getting along with humans: they have been selected rigorously for it over the last fifty thousand years or so. Foxes are not: evolution has nudged them in other, less placid directions. But it's not unreasonable to suggest that foxes have at least the raw mental processing power of dogs. If that's right, by seeing what dogs can do we can get some idea about the resources available to foxes.

Dogs are supreme copiers and bonders. They mimic human actions as well as a sixteen-month-old child, observe closely what humans are looking at or pointing to, read many human social cues, and want to work with us.

Some dogs have capacious memories. One should be careful about drawing conclusions about normality from the spectacular tricks of savants, but the ends of a bell curve do indicate something about where the middle lies. So let's consider a border collie named Rico who appeared on German TV in 2001. He knew the names of two hundred toys, fetched them by name, and learned and remembered words as fast as a human toddler. When a new toy was placed among his old ones he recognized it by a process that must have been something like: "I know the others, but I've never seen this: so this must be the new one." When he'd not seen the new toy for a month, he picked it out correctly in half his trials. The new name had become part of his lexicon: he seemed to slot new words in to some Chomskyite template. Another dog, Betsy, tested in a Hungarian laboratory, had a vocabulary of more than three hundred words.

These capacities and tendencies have obvious emotional (there, I've used the word) corollaries. Dogs suffer separation anxiety when parted from an owner to whom they are bonded. When the owner returns, they race out to greet them, jumping up and dancing, for all the world like a toddler reunited with its mother. Up on the Howden Moors in the Derbyshire

Peak District, where I used to roam as a child, a sheepdog named Tip stayed with the body of his dead master for a desolate, dangerous fifteen weeks.

I can't believe that foxes have used their available RAM in so radically different a way from dogs that these traits have no echoes at all in fox heads. We know that foxes have good memories: they recall, for weeks at a time, not only the location of cached food, but also the particular food that is cached there: "There's a bank vole to the left of the twisted oak; a field vole under the nettles," they say to themselves. We know that they have a significant vocabulary of their own, produced using a sophisticated suite of methods (at least twenty-eight groups of sounds, based on forty basic forms of sound production), and that the call of individual X is recognized as that of individual X rather than of a generic fox: a monogamous captive male reacted only to recordings of his own mate.

These faculties in the fox translate just as inevitably into relationality as the corresponding faculties do in dogs. It's just that the relation, as of course will be the norm with animals (the dog-man case is a highly unusual one), is with other foxes. Who, having heard Macdonald's story of the mutilated vixen, could doubt it?

Here's another of his. A tame dog fox got a thorn in his paw. Septicemia set in. The dominant vixen of his group gave him food when he was ill. That's very unusual: adult foxes are usually aggressively possessive about food.

No doubt this is reciprocal altruism. The vixen, at some level, expected a kickback in the event of her being ill. But that label doesn't begin to mean that there isn't a real emotional component. No doubt my love for my children and the sacrifices I make for them have at least a partial Darwinian explanation. I want them to bear my genes triumphantly on into posterity. But that doesn't mean that I wouldn't be genuinely distressed by their non-reproductive-potential-affecting injury, or that my devastation at their deaths wouldn't go far, far beyond the distress caused by the mere trashing of my genetic aspirations.

I prefer the easy, obvious reading of Macdonald's stories and of the lessons from the dogs. Foxes are relational, empathic creatures. And you can shout "Beatrix Potter" as loudly as you like: I don't care.

This relationality and empathy of fox X is, so far as we know, directed primarily toward other foxes with whom X shares an interest. That's what neo-Darwin says, and no doubt he's right. But once you've got a capacity for relationality and empathy, it's terribly difficult to keep it tidily in its box. It keeps spilling out over other evolutionarily irrelevant individuals and species. People give money to donkeys and to starving children from whom they'll never get any benefit. They even give it secretly, denying themselves the chance of being applauded and favored as a mensch. A Nazi with children of his own will find it harder to bayonet the children of others than one in whom relationality has never kindled.

This is what I told myself, on my knees next to the crane flies and the foxes. Those foxes have the ability to connect to me, and I to them. And there's no reason why they shouldn't want to. There were times (whole seconds at a time) when I've looked at foxes and they've looked at me (in a Yorkshire wood; on a Cornish cliff; in an orange grove near Haifa; on a beach in the Peloponnese), and I've thought: *Yes!* There's a rudimentary language in which we can describe ourselves to the other, and the other to ourselves. We needn't be as mutually inaccessible as Earth and the Baby Boom Galaxy.

Even when those long seconds have passed, I've still been able to say to the fox: Listen, we've both got bodies, and they get wet as the clouds burst on their way up from the gray sea, and we're both *here*! *I* am here! *You* are here!

I and thou!

Then it's usually time to go to the pub.

* * *

When I lived in the East End I'd often give the arrabbiata a miss and shuffle instead at night around the trash cans, rifling through the bags. A fox's nose has no problem telling, through a thick layer of black plastic, whether there's anything worth its while, but even thin plastic defeated mine. I had to open the bags up.

It was only the instinctive phobia of the saliva of my own species that made eating scraps unpleasant. I cheated. I sprinkled mixed spices on everything. That, absurdly, seemed to sterilize it, or at least personalize it and defuse the threat of the dribbling other.

At first I tried caching, the way foxes do. I gave it up in disgust when I returned to a cache of rice in a foil box and found three brown rats with their snouts in it like piglets around a trough. A proper fox would have had them for starters.

The takings were good, but dull. If the East End is like the rest of the Western world, it throws away about a third of all the food it buys. There was no shortage of pizza, chicken tikka masala, egg fried rice, toast, chips, and sausages. But not much else. In this most variegated of all English societies, everyone eats the same as everyone else, and the same all the time. Foxes, even here, do much better than the humans. They have pizza, chicken tikka masala, egg fried rice, toast, chips, sausages, field voles, bank voles, house mice, road casualties of all kinds, wild fruit in season and the air-freighted un-wild, unseasonal fruit of South America and Africa, cockchafer grubs, noctuid moth caterpillars, beetles, rat-tailed maggots from the sewage outlets, earthworms, rabbits (wild and insecurely caged ones), slow complacent birds, rubber bands, broken glass, KFC wrappers, grass to snare intestinal parasitic worms and induce therapeutic vomiting, and just about everything else. But, unfortunately, they're not significant cat killers.

As I mooched around the bins I listened and I watched. I found in the houses and the flats what I found in the bags: uniformity. Everyone had a more or less identical cultural diet. One drizzling September night I stood on the pavement eating an abandoned pie and looking through windows. I could tell from the flickering that seventy-three households were watching TV. Of those, sixty-four (*sixty-four!*), the coordinated flickering told me, were watching the same thing.

No fox ever looks at the same thing as another fox. Even when a family is curled up together, each fox either has its eyes shut, dreaming about chicken houses or a vole glut or an onion *bhaji*, or is looking out from a slightly different angle from every other fox, its understanding of what it's seeing modulated by the slightly different precedence each gives to smell and hearing, with those in turn being conditioned by cement dust in the nose from snuffling around a building site, the angle of the ears, or parental instructions from cubhood.

We, too, have blocked noses and positions in space, but we're such unsensory, unmindful creatures that they make no difference to us: we don't notice them. We have acutely sensitive hands, but we handle the world with thick gloves and then, bored, blame it for lacking shape.

* * *

I'd just about given up on London, but the foxes' faith in it and the intensity of their commitment to it touched me and made me think again. I suspected that if I could get as close to it as they were I'd see it properly, and therefore learn to love it. To hate anything is exhausting. I hoped that the foxes could help me rest.

When I lived here I was almost anesthetic. Like the accursed in the psalm, I had eyes but could not see, a nose but could not smell, hands but could not feel, and ears but could not hear. I was constantly being told that this was where it was all happening, where the real business of life was done. Sometimes I could dimly sense that something *was* happening, but it seemed distant, blurred and muffled, as if I were looking down from a great height through cloudy seawater.

Then, still blind, deaf, and anosmic, I started to follow the foxes. Eventually they took my collar between their teeth and swam with me to four islands. On those islands my senses functioned. I could feel and describe things there. The rest of the Atlantean world of the East End remained submerged. If I'd stayed longer, and persevered with the foxes, they might have shown me more islands, or perhaps even dived down with me, or raised the rest of Atlantis so that I could buy and taste beer in it, or run over its hills and feel it under my feet.

I never got anywhere other than the islands, and never really understood what made the East End tick. Perhaps the genius loci lies deep in the troughs between my islands, forever out of my reach. Yet in describing my islands to myself I mapped an archipelago, and an archipelago has a taste of its own: it can be a nation of which one can be fond.

I wanted most of all to feel fond. I was so tired of resenting. If I thought that fondness for a place was different from understanding the foxes that inhabit the place, I'd want the fondness more than the understanding. But the conviction that they weren't different had grown with every sniff and crawl and trash bag raid.

It wasn't that I experienced something on the islands that was better than anesthesia elsewhere but not as good as normal experience. Not at all. I became convinced that the foxes saw, smelled, and heard the real thing, and that on the islands to which they took me I was experiencing the real thing, too. The foxes gave me their eyes, ears, noses, and feet. But only on the islands.

The foxes were the real East Enders. They inhabited the place in a way that, without their help, I could not, and in a way that reflected what the place itself was. I lived there in a way that reflected me, or my view of the place. I walked around with a mirror in front of me, describing myself into a notebook and calling it nature writing.

If you look into a fox's eyes, you get no reflection of yourself. They have vertical pupils, which deny gratification to the human narcissist. Now jump to the other side of the fox's eye and look out through it at a pool of vomited curry, or a hedgehog, or a stream of 4x4s on the school run. You'll similarly get no reflection of yourself. You'll see the things themselves, or a better approximation to the things than you'd get with your own drearily self-referential eyes. Eyes are meant to be sensory receptors. In the fox's head they are. We make them cognitive, and ruin them. This is not because a fox has less consciousness and hence there is less to intrude between its retina and its mental model of that hedgehog, but because its consciousness is less contaminated with toxic self and presumption.

None of the fox islands was visible from more than two feet above the ground. One could be seen only with the nose.

These are the islands.

ISLAND 1

There are lots of shops that sell everything, deep into the night. They smell of ghee, soap, cardamom, coriander, and lighter fuel. The owners never ever die or get excited. In an alleyway beside one of these there was a pile of crates stamped with customs ink from Barbados and Bangladesh and some little piles of Pacific rock. It was soft, sweet, damp, and alcoholic under the crates. I floated on a raft of fermenting fruit. The wasps were too pissed to sting me when I rolled on them.

I lay on my belly, because foxes normally do. There was a

wall a couple of feet ahead of me. Damp had edged up the first foot. The rest of the wall, which climbed up to the billowing net-curtain-sails of a taxi firm's masthead, was dry as toast, and as interesting. But next to the ground there was writhing wonderment: silver slug tracery; trundling woodlice, swimming through air as baby trilobites rowed through the Cambrian soup; centipedes armored in bronze plates, snaking like a file of legionnaires with shields over their heads toward a tower of hairy Goths; lichens flowering the way that scabs would flower if skin healing were directed by William Morris; moss like armpit hair.

A crack in a box from Lesotho half-framed a bathroom window, and the woman in the bathroom was lovely and the man was not. Why would she stay? But that was not a fox thought. If I lowered my head there was a cauliflower, green with mold and bonny as a horse chestnut in May.

There were worms in the raft, fat, pickled worms with thick saddles like the thick wedding rings of the emphatically faithful. A fox would have sucked them through its teeth like spaghetti: each is worth 2½ calories—one two hundred and fortieth of the six-hundred-calorie-per-day requirement of an adult fox. Although most foxes eat some earthworms, it seems that some are worm specialists, to judge by the soil and worm *chetae* in their dung. It's a safe, lazy way to earn a living, like being a probate lawyer.

ISLAND 2

In the park there's a place where concrete meets asphalt. The concrete has broken where the winter has hardened water into wedges. There's a lush tree of cracks. Flash floods, invisible to us, but tumultuous wild water to greenfly, have filled the cracks with soil, full of ascarid eggs from unbagged dog shit near the playground. Wind, shoveled by the side view mirrors of cement trucks and white vans, has seeded the soil with grass, and bravely straggling ragwort whose ancestors probably killed a horse or two in Kent.

If you walk on this boundary with bare feet, you'll know that the concrete is as hard and sharply pitted as a cheese grater. It doesn't welcome anything. The sun leaves it as fast as it can go. The asphalt, though, is warm and spongy, even in the cold. When it's hot it sends up tar tendrils to grab your feet. They leave tattoos, like black thread veins, on your soles.

Foxes have absurdly sensitive feet. These city foxes, used to pounding the roads for eight hours a night, have pads that feel like velvet that has had milk poured over it and then been put in the oven overnight to get a fragile crust. Their feet, like their faces, extend beyond the fur line: there are small, stiff hairs on the carpus that are buried in a buzzing hive of nerves. When the biologist Huw Lloyd lightly touched these hairs on a young fox sleeping in front of his fire, the fox, without waking, snatched back its foot. Those hairs are stroked lustfully by the grass in any country wilder than a well-managed sports field. Imagine your nostrils being shafted enjoyably with face-high thistles as you walk. That's a fox's progress through a spring wood.

It seems a bit much. They really don't need to be so good. Clumping, club-footed ungulates, their nerve endings locked up in horn boxes, dance perfectly satisfactorily over rough ground and along mountain ledges. You'd expect natural selection to be more parsimonious in dispensing its favors to foxes.

ISLAND 3

We think of small trees as going straight up from the ground, and then getting wider like mushrooms or narrower like carrots. They don't. Even the slenderest tree has a big, wide underground life. The parts up in the light are just kitchens for making food.

If you lie on the ground you'll eventually know this. I watched one tree for about three hours before noticing. It had sloping shoulders, hinting at a pale body beneath the paving.

The tree prized up the stiff skin of the yard, and then, tired, slumped onto the fence, pulled down by the weight of its head as a drunk's head is pulled onto a table by the weight of a headful of beer. Ants, beetles, and earwigs, each in their own rigidly observed carriageways, poured over the shoulders—streams of iridescent water with legs. They were going to eat dead stuff, or live stuff: it's always one or the other. The boundary between the two isn't very clear.

I couldn't gallop between trees on my hands and knees in the East End. There aren't enough trees. But I've done it as best I can in plenty of other places. The real fox's-eye view of trees is when you're sledding fast downhill through woodland. Foxes have, like most predators, frontally positioned eyes. They'd have had more or less the same view of the beetles as I had, but I'd have been able to identify the tree species at a running speed sooner than the foxes. For them the trees would have been dark columns that would have come at them with that lurching, not-quite-anticipatable violence that you know best when you're driving one of those fake motorbikes in an amusement arcade. Computer simulation of driving or riding doesn't feel like driving or riding, but it's useful for making you feel like a fox.

I tried to run like a fox at the tree in the yard. I skinned my knees, and the woman in the house next door pulled back her curtain and asked nervously if I was all right.

ISLAND 4

I turned over an old slice of pizza with my nose. It was lying in a backyard. I don't know how it had escaped the rats and the birds and the foxes. It had lasted long enough to have soaked up the weather of a couple of weeks. There had been no rain for a week, but it was damp. There was a luxurious green fur over the pepperoni. There were human tooth marks on one side, and the fur was thinner there: presumably the streptococci of which human kisses are a concentrated solution compete viciously with the mold. The underside was a metro system, its tunnels already packed, like a rush-hour station, with jostling weevils. Black beetles (which I always think are too downright mechanical to need food—which is a demand of flesh) were there directing the crowds.

But it was the smell that got me. There were physical smell strata in the slice: at the top there was still metallic tomato and the fat of unhappy pigs, shaken up with spores (which don't smell at all of death, though they should). At the bottom there was pasty, yeasty creepingness. The tomato and the metro were separated by about an inch (it was a deep-pan pizza) and a fortnight. But—and this was the point—I got them both in a single sniffing millisecond.

Smell telescopes and packages history. The pizza was a trivial example. Sniff a lump of Precambrian schist and you might get a couple of billion years of sensation delivered all at once to your neurological door. The sensation, in that case, will be faint: most of the scent molecules will have been reassigned to other bodies and structures, and those that remain are wrapped tightly in a sort of archaic cling film.

As a fox trots down the Bethnal Green Road, it takes with every breath an instantaneous transect through the past five or fifty or five hundred years. And it lives in those years, rather than on the tarmac and between the bins. Time, squashed tightly by olfaction, is the fox's real geography.

The piece of pizza wasn't substantial enough to be an island itself. It was a signpost—a floating piece of fresh wood that said an island wasn't far off. The island from which it came was a tree stump crumbling and spongy, next to a ruptured trash bag. Like litmus, it had soaked up the runoff from the bag, and like litmus it declared the real nature of the bag and the bag's ancestors. The declaration was in the smell, and the nature was historical and anthropological and commercial and depraved and careless and anxious and just about all the other adjectives there are. *And I got it all at once.*

I think it had been a lime tree, but its own name had been chewed by the rain and the wasps and washed out by curry bleeding from the bag. Because it was porous, it was a safe and capacious bank of the memory of things. Perhaps it was planted a century ago, for no reason that the planners would have been able to explain: there wasn't language then for motives like "feeding the wild heart beating inside the black jacket." And it died about half a century later when its varicose roots were hacked because they made next door's yard too interesting.

When it died, it started to accumulate scent. When it was alive it had mostly smelled of itself.

I moved the bag and slept by the tree for a couple of nights, with my nose in one of its armpits.

That nose went through three stages. First, it smelled an old tree and molded its scent into the shape of a cadaver. Then the nose laid the scent out and (it's a big, sharp nose) began to dissect. It cut out a slice of diesel, perhaps from the mid-seventies, and put that in a bowl for later inspection. Then the nose went back, picked up a length of storm blown in from Russia at the time of the Suez crisis, and laid it alongside. With those out of the way, it speeded up: last month's menstrual blood, a brave crack at cheering up a nursery, an overambitious and unpopular attempt at a Vietnamese culinary classic, some evidently successful attempts at safe sex. And beans. So many beans. All laid out in the bowl.

The nose roved around the bowl from item to item, proud of its dissection.

And then, very slowly, it began to know that it is murder

to dissect. It reassembled the pieces. It got again what it had got in the first, unexamined sniff, the whole bowl at once, a century in a moment.

That, I think, is how a fox does it. But it inhabits a much longer period in a moment than I can, and inhabits that period far more fully. Yes, it focuses on the things it's particularly interested in, as I lock onto one alluring picture in a new gallery. But it sweeps the millennia in an instant, as my eye sweeps the gallery. From the millennia the fox alights on last week's chops or the last minute's vole, but the scan is complete.

Only noses can travel in time quite like this. Our eyes and ears travel, too, but we don't recognize it, because light and sound are so fast. We see the light from stars that are centuries old, and the light is mixed on the palette of our retina with light that is tiny fractions of a nanosecond old from the nearby fast food joint. We use the mixture to paint a picture of the world that we call reality. In fact, reality's a cocktail of sometimes radically different times, shaken and profoundly stirred by the Self.

So those were my islands: a fruit raft, the edge of some concrete, a tree, and a stump. Foxes took me there.

As a matter of mere aesthetics I preferred the fox view to my view from the bus or from my study. It was prettier and much more interesting. As a matter of cartography I came to think that the fox view of the East End was more accurate than mine: it took into account more information. It saw both more minutely and more widely. It saw the hairs on ants' legs and, in a moment-to-moment orgy of olfactory holism, everything that had been spilled, ejaculated, cooked, and grown since the creation of the world. So there.

The foxes showed me a London that was old and deep enough to live in and be kind about. They negotiated an uneasy peace between me and the East End, and indeed between me and other squalid, wretched, broken human places. It was a great gift.

But I'd gotten to know only islands, not whole landscapes.

The city squirmed mistily below the waters between them. For my metaphorically maritime foxes there is no mistiness.

* * *

Time travel isn't just poetry. Foxes use it for hunting. If a vole squeaks from any point to one side of a fox's midline, the sound hits the fox's eardrums at slightly different times, and at slightly different intensities. A bit of basic trigonometry, a lot of experience, and a lot of wasted pounces, and the brain will have a rough fix. Although it's more difficult (as evolution, on behalf of pure-toned prey species, has noted), even a continuous, pure-toned moan can be located: a different part of the wave reaches each ear at a particular time—a crest might smash into the right, and a trough into the left. The discrepancies locate the squeaker or the moaner. But only up to a point. If the fox keeps its head still, the sound will be localized not to one dot in space, but to a graceful curved plane, starting at the moan and ending over the fox's head. In its killing leap, the fox can't chop every point along that plane. It has to do better, and it does, in two ways.

First, it moves its head or its ears. The plane linking the moan to the fox moves, but the moan doesn't. By comparing the original plane with the new one, the fox can narrow the possibilities. Several ear swivelings or head swings later, there will be almost enough confidence to justify that costly spring. But there's another astonishing refinement.

To appreciate how astonishing this is, go out to the most disgusting park you know and watch dogs defecating. On a normal day, they prefer to defecate with their bodies aligned along the north-south axis. That's when the earth's magnetic field is calm. It's not always calm: there are storms and squalls as the molten rock we're all surfing on churns around. But given a quiet day in Hades, our dogs' bowels are tethered to the center of the world.

We don't know if foxes do this, but it's likely. They're certainly tuned to the earth's magnetic field. They very significantly prefer to leap in a northeasterly direction onto those small mammals, and are much more likely to kill if they do. There's a death in 73 percent of northeasterly jumps, in 60 percent of southwesterly jumps (at 180 degrees to the preferred direction), and in only 18 percent of jumps in other directions.

What they're doing (and it's the only known instance—so far—of animals doing this) is using the field to calculate distance rather than position or direction. That's rather important. Many things confound distance finding in the fox's normal habitat. The speed of sound varies with air temperature and humidity, skewing those trigonometrical calculations. Sound slaloms between grass stems, bounces off twigs, insinuates into the ground, and frolics off in the wind. On well-trodden vole paths there's rarely a telltale sway of grass, and if there is, a breeze will cover the tracks. Over or undershooting is wasteful: there may well not be a chance to regroup and refire.

So the fox jumps at a fixed angle to the magnetic field (ideally twenty degrees off magnetic north). It knows the angle of the sound reaching its ears. Where the magnetic line and the sound line meet, there meat will be. Remember how the Dambusters knew when to drop the bouncing bomb on the Ruhr dams? When the two spotlights met on the surface of the water, they knew that they were the right distance from the wall, and they pressed the release button. That's what foxes do, but one spotlight is sound, and the other is magnetic, and the release is an explosive unfolding of hamstrings and about a hundred or so other muscles filled with blood, lymph, and hunger.

What might it be like to take one's bearings so literally from the earth? I fix sounds as foxes do, moving my head. But to feel northwesterliness in your water? That would give every step a context—a relatedness to everything else. It would make me a true citizen of the world, rather than of the patch I happen to be fouling at the time.

Once I sat in a pub listening to some elderly ladies talking about how the world was going downhill. Young people, of course, weren't what they used to be. But in an interesting respect. It wasn't that they were idle, unwashed, promiscuous, disrespectful, or intoxicated—although they were. It was that they were overly sensitive to magnetic fields.

"They think, you know, that churches and that are all stuck along magnetic lines. Joined to old hills and the like."

"They don't!"

"They do. Let me tell you. They say that there are lines of power all over the country, and that people in the olden days used to know about them, and built things on them."

"They never!"

"They do. Wonder if I'm on one now. Me bum's tingling."

And so it went on: bums and then breasts tingled; shapeless pants were mockingly electrified; the feng shui of mantelpiece junk from Benidorm was evaluated. It cackled into the night as I bought narcotic beer I hadn't thought I'd need, and tried to knuckle down to *Greenmantle*.

Their despised grandchildren were right; ask any fox, bushman, squatting dog, or just about anyone before the dark dawn of modernity. Magnetism, along with burial and planting, anchors humans to the planet. We are alphabetic fridge magnets: our only hope of spelling something coherent is to hang on. To be unmagnetic in the Upper Paleolithic was to be blind and footless. You wouldn't know, properly, or intimately, where you were. And hence why and who you were.

Or so I wrote, self-righteously and adolescently, in my beer-stained notebook. I was no more magnetic than the women.

My ancestors, just as much as theirs, had hacked off their own feet and put out their own eyes sometime in the last thousand years. But at least I didn't think it made them or me better.

Perhaps I'm overstating things. When a fox uses the angle of twenty degrees off magnetic north for efficient killing, it's not doing it any more transcendentally than a Ping-Pong player turning her wrist for maximum topspin. But not less transcendentally, either. Which makes me conclude, on balance, that I'm not overstating. For the connection between a world class Ping-Pong player and the table is surely a wondrous thing. For me, the table is a piece of wood. For the player, it's a stage on which extraordinary things can happen, a frame on which embroidery of unique beauty can be woven. That's possible only because of the connection between the player and the table.

So the whole world, for unmagnetic me, is as far below what it might be as a few planks of wood are below a table used for an international table tennis tournament. Foxes play Ping-Pong all day and all night.

* * *

The churchyards and canal banks of this part of the East End were too tidy. There were voles there, but I needed longer grass to hunt them. I needed to swim breaststroke through the grass until I found their paths, which are chlorophyll cloisters. Then I could stand and hover over them like a hunting kestrel.

Foxes can leap up to ten feet horizontally, from a standing start, in order to pinion a vole. (That's like me jumping about twenty-six feet.) They jump high, too—perhaps to get a better view of the hunting field, just as a human deerstalker climbs to a high point to scope the ground—though the fox has a specific target on its auditory and magnetic screens and just needs some fine-tuning for the final approach.

There was no need for me to jump high when I was vole

hunting. My eyes were naturally far above the zenith of the most athletic fox's leap. My ears were useless. Mice (and probably voles) can squeak at a wide variety of frequencies, from those audible to my ears to well into what we call the ultrasonic range. Foxes do much better than I at the high frequencies. They perform best at around 3,500 cycles per second, which is where I do well, too. (Human ears are most sensitive at around 1,000 to 3,500 Hz, but they are amazing audiological all-arounders: they can locate sounds accurately in more than 90 percent of cases in the range of 900–14,000 Hz, and even at 34,000 Hz—well beyond even the youngest of us—they get it right around two thirds of the time.)

The fox's technique is thus: reconnoiter (know where the vole cloisters are): listen for a squeak; move head and/or ears to get a cross-bearing; supplement if necessary by listening for a lower frequency and thus more accessible noise, like the rustling of a dry leaf; fix magnetic distance; jump; minute visual correction; kill.

My technique was: reconnaissance; stand astride the cloister: watch for a grass blade moving or listen for a rustle; drop suddenly and hopefully, landing with my face in a pile of vole dung; miss; brush myself off; try pointlessly to explain myself to the group of concerned citizens clustered anxiously nearby; make off before police arrive.

I've spent hours doing this. It became an obsession. I never got near, and I never got better. About five times out of several hundred leaps I saw my prey—sidling arrogantly, mockingly away. One of them actually turned around. You wouldn't have thought that, anatomically, a vole could sneer. But it can. I know.

The life of small mammals is written in Morse: dots and dashes. They dash between the dots. They pause, trembling between the dashes—so more of a semicolon than a dot—to conduct a detailed assessment of the situation.

I've just come back from watching shrews on the riverbank. They rush for a couple of seconds; wait for three; rush for two; wait for three; and so on. And in the waits they are wondering how to make it across the next foot of leaf litter, and perhaps (it's not such a big step) whether they'll make it.

Most predators become their prey, or at least adopt their rhythm. But foxes don't do that. There's no staccato in a fox. They manage to be themselves more than any other animal I know. They make no concession to the prey or the place. A fox from the churning gut of a city lives about as long as one from a beech wood or a mountain. It'll insist on needlessly hunting, and it won't die of coronary artery disease. It'll carry on being foxy, whereas thoroughly urbanized humans are in danger of not being optimally human.

Urban foxes' foxiness is all the more spectacular because they spend so much of their time badly injured—by vehicles, of course. It's a consequence of their confident foxiness. Why should they run from such strange predators? The road is their home; why should they move? Rumble and light don't impress them into fear or flight.

A heroic experiment demonstrated just how much pain is stirred into the mix of bristling alarm and poised command that is the brief but dazzling life of a city fox. The hero scraped up more than three hundred dead foxes from the streets of London and laid them out for the flies. Several months later, and probably many friends lighter, he could see that 27.5 percent of them had healed fractures—most of them, no doubt, from hurtling lumps of steel propelled by decomposed plants from carboniferous forests.

We can't know how foxes cope mentally with the disruption of their bodies, but I've seen lots of dogs look, puzzled, at the splintered ends of bone coming out of their legs. They soon start licking the ends, as they'd lick a new puppy. They deal with the mystery of one bloody thing erupting out of their bodies as they deal with other bloody eruptions. They welcome it into the air.

I've looked at the splintered ends of my bones. I didn't welcome them. Tubes sprayed blood into my eyes until, unbidden, the tubes pinched themselves off. We're always and only kept alive by unbidden things. Put a heart cell onto a glass slide and it'll keep contracting in time to the baton of a dead conductor who never even knew he was conducting.

Foxes aren't just run down by vehicles: they're run down by time, too. Thirty-five percent of London foxes have spondylosis deformans—a deforming fusion of their joints—most commonly in their spines. Sixty-five percent of foxes in their third year of life have arthritis in their spines: all of the few who survive to the grand old age of six do. When they walk along fence tops like teenage Romanians on the Olympic beam, or blast from a hedge onto a wood pigeon, or seep like mercury up to a rabbit, they're doing it with a back so bad that, were they office workers, it would have them signed permanently off work. They must look forward to lying under the shed during the day, and must see the approaching of the night with the same resigned dread with which a man more committed to his office than to his crippling sciatica hears the morning alarm.

* * *

Beneath the roof of my den, for day after long, long day, I dozed, hot, shivering, fitful: never right. The view I commanded was the view that a fox under the shed would have had. I had no sky. At this low altitude, horizontal perspectives are steep: a drainpipe funneled the world fast into a vanishing point. Vertical perspectives, though, are sickening. Once your eyes are raised from the ground there is only wall. We live in a well: light drips in from the top through an invisible mesh of cloud and fumes.

We don't know much about the color perception of foxes, but it's likely that they are red-green color-blind. Here, though, it doesn't make much difference. These humans, thinking that flowers are vulgarly overdone, have opted for gray—or at least that's what the prevailing westerlies and the drip-fed sun disdainfully do to their pastels after a season.

When a fox, after playing with its vole for a while, as my children roll their peas around the plate, snips off its head, the blood is just a darker shade of gray on the gray grass.

I wallowed incontinently under that groundsheet, chapped and stinking, watching and listening.

My watching wasn't so unlike the fox's. At short ranges, in the day, its visual acuity was more or less as good as mine, but its eyes needed rather more tickling than mine to become interested.

The central area of its retina is dominated by cones rather than rods, and cones are much better at detecting movement than they are at recognizing shapes. A baby rabbit, well within the fox's field of vision at noon, is likely to be safe as long as it stays still. A man with a gun, raising himself slowly, slowly, slowly on his arms, will be likely, even when he's silhouetted against the skyline, to kill that daytime fox. The silhouette will (not imperceptibly, but unperceived) become part of the background noise in the fox's brain; it's filtered out, leaving attention only for new eruptions of sound.

My daytime eyes are better at shapes than the fox's, and my brain is also more interested in them. Though the boredom of the days was crushing, there was more entertainment for me than for the fox. I didn't need a beetle or a fast-swinging shadow, though they were appreciated. I could make do with a pinecone, a frill of lichen, or the Corinthian fluting of an iron trash can.

My round pupils were made for wonder; for invasion by

the world; for allowing takeover by all comers. It's only my brain, made timid and conservative by the last few millennia, that checks the credentials of everyone at the door, letting in only the familiar and unthreatening.

A fox presumably puts fewer cognitive obstacles in the way of the world. It's governed more by the physics of its pupils. At night they're round, as mine always are: then, it needs all the clues the woods and the streets can offer. In the day the pupils are more skeptical and discriminating: upright slits, like erect sentries, which are much better at keeping light out. They work with the eyelids to titrate exactly the optimal amount of visible world.

The fox and I heard some of the same things: we both heard punches landing (the fox would have wondered if there'd be a corpse for supper); and people being hysterically cheerful on the radio; and disembodied chopping, grinding, grating, rumbling, whirring, and pinging. All of this was interesting to me; almost none of it to the fox. For her, nothing much above her head was worth attention. She'd evolved so as not to fear aerial predation (the most powerful eagle isn't much threat), and the occasional deadly blast from the bedroom window of a farmhouse isn't so significant as to nudge evolution toward dread of a thunderous sky god. So she would have noted and immediately discarded (with the sort of mindfulness at which I've worked, cross-legged, cramped, and unsuccessfully, for years), the soft crackling of poplars (you hear the cracks only after a couple of hours), the myocardial thump of a power washer, the scrappy scratch and trill of starlings in the house's voicebox under the eaves.

For her, though, the stir of dry leaves by the compost heap, which was for me a nibbling, was like sharp fingernails scraping down a drum held hard against the ear. Her attention would move from the general (or the general below five feet) to the leaves, just as the attention of one of those accomplished meditators clicks back and locks onto the breath.

* * *

I did most of my foxery before I had small cubs. It seemed fun at the time. Now it would be even more fun, and I'd see a lot more. They'd peel the scales off my eyes, and there would be vertical pupils beneath. Human children are more like fox kits than they're like anything else. Mine even cache like foxes (there are little piles of gummy bears behind books and under carpets), and for the same reasons (small stomachs and an apocalyptic imagination that subliminally tells them, against all the evidence, that there won't be food tomorrow).

Their memory for the caches seems to be about as good and as bad as the fox's.

Weeks 1 and 2: "Where did you leave those gummy bears?" "Behind the Lego bucket."

Week 3: "Behind the lego bucket? I think. Or perhaps by the penis gourds?"

Week 4: "What gummy bears? Please: what gummy bears?"

When they had to excavate, though, the memory was buried more safely in their heads. We buried cans of beans and tomatoes up on Exmoor, and though they were a lot less interesting than candy, the children remembered the location perfectly three months later—though their ability to remember which can was where was down to fox/candy level in a fortnight.

I don't want them to change. They have nothing that they don't need in order to live properly, and they lack nothing. In that, too, they're like foxes. I fear their evolution—fear particularly that it will be assimilation into a less intimate world, a world in which sensitivity is impossible.

I fear that too for the red foxes of the inner city, although there is encouragingly little sign of it. If it were going to happen, there might well be signs of it already. Genetics and evolution, coupled together, make a fast and powerful machine. But they are still at risk. When, for a mere forty generations, traits of friendliness to humans were artificially selected in silver foxes, those cold, snarling pots of poison barked, wagged their tails, whimpered cravenly when humans walked toward them, and licked human hands.

May God or Darwin protect my children from comparable breeding.

* * *

I hate cats. Really hate them. This isn't the dispassionate distaste that everyone who likes birds, small mammals, and relationality should have. It's elemental, wholly disproportionate to the damage they do, and getting worse by the year.

Nobody really likes cats as cats. They're intrinsically unlikable: vain, cold, and cruel. To like a cat you've got to turn it into something that it plainly isn't. You have to dress it up as a lover, a postmistress, or an old school chum. Cats are at their best in the hands of a really bad taxidermist.

I don't wish them ill: I just unwish them. I'm religiously committed to the removal of their reproductive apparatus. It's very disappointing that only 0.4 percent of Oxford urban fox scats contain cat fur—and probably most of that is from roadkilled cats.

The smell of cat urine enrages me. I don't know which came first—hatred of cats or hatred of their urine—and now I can't disentangle the two. But when a tomcat sprayed the tarp that was the roof of my fox den, terrible things happened to my head.

I put a chicken leg on the sheet and wriggled underneath. It wasn't long before I felt the cat climb up my back. The chicken was on my shoulder. I wanted to smash that insolent composure. I waited until I knew the cat would have his teeth in the leg, then erupted skyward with a Vesuvian roar. There was a gratifying screech, and the cat shot up and off with neuroses that would be immune to all the veterinary CBT money could buy.

I chased him across the yard, to the end of what we laughingly called the garden. He jumped over some planks. So did I. He cleared a flowerpot. So did I. He leaped onto a fence and ran along it. So did I. He did so with balletic elegance. I did not.

I fell between a wall and a shed, slumped, panting, and swearing. I was there for a minute. I looked up into vertical pupils in a sharp red head, six feet away. The chicken leg drooped out of one corner of her mouth, for all the world like a cheroot. She held my gaze: it was certainly her holding mine, not me holding hers. Then, when she chose, she let me go, strolled to the corner of the yard, and left through a door that wasn't there.

* * *

Foxes gave London back to me for a while. They would have given me more if I'd asked. But it seemed unfair to press them. They had other things to do in the few smoothly bristling seasons that the statistics allowed them. I had nothing to give them. They didn't need me, my domestic waste, my sympathy, or my fantasies of wild companionship. That needlessness, and the memory of smiling eyes above a chicken cheroot, gave me the only confidence I have that it's all going to be all right.

5. RED DEER

Red deer are designed to be hunted by wolves.

It is easy enough to be a wolf. This is how I did it.

First, I was born into a society that baaed: "Acquisition good; renunciation bad." Then I went to a school brazen enough to have compulsory lessons in laissez-faire economics called "Community Wealth," and where on Tuesday afternoons we looked through the sights of Second World War Lee Enfield rifles at charging Communists and got splendid badges for nailing them between the eyes.

Then I went to an ancient university that was ancient, the stones and the occasional drunken don told us, because in every generation excellence came to the top by a natural law of anti-gravity and mingled eugenically with more excellence to create still more excellence. And so it would continue until the world was filled with the glory of Adam Smith, as the waters covered the sea. After six years of mediocrity I was invited for dry sherry in an oak-paneled room overlooking the Cam. A Fellow of the Royal Society in a black gown asked us to sit down.

"You're about to leave Cambridge, gentlemen. Now, it may very well be true that the meek will inherit the earth, but my advice to you is this: Until they show some signs of making a serious bid for that position, trample all over them."

Thus equipped, we strode out into the world. Or, in my case, slunk out, wolf now by constitution, but not by conviction.

You need a revolution to change a constitution, and for a long time I was too busy for that. I tooled myself up to carry on the baton of wolfishness. That meant professional scalps, papers, girls, and guns. And, preeminently, it meant the sleeper train from Euston to the hunting grounds of Inverness or Fort William in September.

I loved it. I love it still. There's a gratifying apartheid in the restaurant car. It's not safe to leave your rifle in your sleeping compartment, so it's got to be with you as, eating your microwaved haggis, you look pityingly at the unarmed tourists eating salad. There's a tense priapic fellowship between the stalkers: we despise the others even more than we dislike and distrust one another. We raise our eyebrows as an aspirational peasant who doesn't know the rules asks for Glenfiddich (because he's seen it in an in-flight mag) instead of an island malt. We silently and companionably mock their practical waterproof coats, their light, breathable trousers, their easily tied boots, and particularly their earnestness. They've all got their maps out. They're tapping grid references into their GPSs and calculating the distances between huts. But we: we have no need of navigation. We go where we bloody well want and kill the deer that we bloody well want to kill. We don't mention to ourselves that we don't take maps because we'll be shepherded on the hill by a professional stalker who despises us far more than even we are capable of despising these kind, hardy, self-reliant walkers who probably do triathlons in the time it takes us to drink a pint of overpriced beer at the White Horse on Parsons Green. No, we're the wolves;

they're the deer. We eat them. Good on 'em for playing the part and eating spinach.

By the time the train has lurched into the north Midlands the tourists have trotted down the corridor to early beds. Very wise: you never know when they'll have to run to escape one of us.

Before they turned in, things were simple: there were wolves and there were prey. Now, though, we have a closer look at the other wolves; leaders, soon-to-be leaders, and followers. That's a brand-new gun case; bet he's not seen much action. He won't get a good look at a stag's heart through those owlish glasses when the fog's coming down. And look at those arms: they'll never hold a rifle steady when he's waited three hours in the cold for a stag to get up. The girl's pretty enough, but there's too much of the bottle about that hair for her to get a return invite to the table in our lodge. And I bet she can't sing, play, recite, or otherwise do her bit in the drawing room after dinner.

Self-deception isn't always possible. In my mind at least, there's usually someone in the corner, laconic and ironic, drinking water and tea, a very battered rifle propped up beside him, dressed in faded clothes, desert boots insolently on the seat, reading Sophocles in the original, and perfectly happy to kill and eat me.

By Fort William the distinctions between the wolves have been ground down by the turning wheels. Only the natural aristocracy of the smiling Sophoclean remains, as immutable as the mutability of the highland weather. We're disgorged, crumpled, stiff, and fearful, into old Land Rovers.

Because there are wolves and wolves, there are lodges and lodges. Some (think Germans, Americans, and complex, agented rental agreements) have tartan carpets and wallpaper, immaculate gravel, a flat screen TV, and *jus*. And others have cheese safes, a barrel of beer in the kitchen, a wood-fired drying room, and gravy. I've only ever killed from this second kind, may Diana be thanked.

The breakfasts are leisurely, and fittingly carnivorous. Then there may be a ride in a boat down the loch to a remote beach for an amphibious start to the campaign (which was of course how we talked about it), or a jolting journey around the hill to kinder wind, or a spy from the hedges and a crawl within sight of the kitchen windows.

In my wolf years I killed many deer with my exploding teeth. I don't know how many. I never kept a diary. Sometimes I thought that to chronicle the days would preserve them, and so allow me to keep living in them, and hence keep me from living effectively in them as they were happening. And sometimes I thought that a mere account of my doings would so radically miss the point of what was going on that it wasn't worth it.

Just what *was* going on I wasn't clear about. I'm still not. But there was, even then, something shameful about it. It wasn't the unfairness—knocking over a beast seen through a telescopic sight at three hundred yards when I would never have been able to spear it. It wasn't the fact of the killing, as that fact is represented in the estate's ledger: a certain number of deer have to be killed. It had something to do with relationship, and hence with proximity and with those telescopic three hundred yards. I was doing a terrible, intimate, undoable thing; I was molding an ecosystem. I was ending something and beginning something else. And I wasn't even there to take hands-on responsibility for it: a finger on a trigger is not a hand. I wasn't there to see what it meant when a bullet zigzagged through the thorax, ricocheting off ribs and ripping blood vessels. I wasn't there to apologize; to explain; to shoulder the burden of regret that is also the burden of exultation. A stag is fearfully and wonderfully made. I had carelessly and easily unmade it. To un-create is (I suppose my logic went) an un-godly thing to do. I began to know why the kosher laws preserve, in their horror of blood, the old, unhistorical insistence that we were all vegetarians once, that we had the relationship then with nonhuman animals that we need for our own thriving. Standing on the hill by a shattered stag, I was as ontologically queasy as a Hasid who's had a mouthful of black pudding. I felt dirty, and I didn't want smutty literary photos of me lying around in a drawer to snigger at later.

Because there was no diary, there is now just the memory of a generic stalk; a chimera woven from many strands, from many hills. But the strands that make up the red deer's story are only from red deer: there are no roe deer, or zebra, or wildebeest, or blesbok, or hartebeest strands in there. It's not true the other way around. There are some coarse brown highland hairs from Conaglen deer coloring the zebra. Red deer are special. They are more themselves than the other ungulates I've killed. They're more jealous of the specialness of their deaths.

This (excluding the crucial details of lusts, lunches, and of course misses) is how the red deer stalk goes.

You go to a target in front of some sandbags. A thin man in tweed looks skeptically at you unless and until you can put three bullets within two inches of one another at two hundred yards. If you can't, it's time to get back on the train. There's no point in continuing to exist, and life, if it continues at all, will never be the same again. You are not a predator.

If you can, the thin man nods at you and puts the rifle back in its slip, and you walk together to the hill. Your relief about the target will make you want to talk companionably. That wouldn't be appreciated. You might be a predator, but you're right at the bottom of the pack pyramid.

That thin stalker, anyway, has things to do. He's scanning the hill as you walk. You do, too, but it's not the same. You try to look acute and farsighted, sometimes stopping and leaning forward sagely to look at a fold by a corrie, but no one's taken in.

You both stop. The stalker takes out his binoculars. You take out yours. You both sweep the hill. The stalker says: "Two nice stags, but a parcel of hinds in front. We'll never get through to them." You pretend that you can see them, nod. He picks up some grass and throws it away to see what the wind is doing. He sweeps the hill again, sucks his teeth. He sits down on a tussock, pulls out a brass telescope, puts it to his eye, steadies it on his knee. "There's a shootable stag at the foot of the scree," he says. "We might get there."

There is now, although it's not spelled out, a sophisticated plan. You climb into a gully that goes up to the ridge. The wind is blowing from the deer to you, and you are out of sight, so this part can be fast, and should be. Weather can drop fast; deer can be spooked by anything and nothing.

You have to get out of the gully before it meets the ridge. An old sentinel hind has the shape of the skyline running constantly in her head just as you might have a tune running in yours. You'd notice a small change in the melody, or even a mildly distorted chord. So will she. So you climb out of the trench and into no-man's-land. There's no need yet to crawl. "But keep down," says the stalker, and you walk slowly, bent double. The stalker stops, and you, a pace behind, desperate to please, cannon into him. He reaches around and grabs your jacket, keeping you behind him. The hind has looked up and at him. She's not happy. She keeps looking at him for a tense minute. Then she puts her head down and continues feeding. The stalker doesn't move, and quite right: a few seconds later the hind whips her head up again and looks straight at you. It's an old trick. The first gaze didn't satisfy her. She hopes that if there's anything suspicious it will have thought that she was reassured, will have started to move again, and will be caught by the second look. This happens a few times between now and the scree slope. You have to see the swing of the neck and stop moving before the eyes lock on.

The stag's grazing at the foot of the slope. He relies on the women for protection. About three hundred yards from the stag there's an area of rough grass. It's a mixed blessing: it might cover the final crawl, but it might also baffle a bullet. Between you and the grass there's precious little cover for another three hundred yards.

You get flat on your face, with your genitals scraping the ground. Many a stag has been saved by a proud, disobedient arse. The idea is to go at the speed of continental drift, since if the deer are themselves floating at the same speed, their movement-detecting software won't be activated.

A raven, looking for carrion, sees you and stoops low for a better look. He sees your hand inching forward and veers away. The hind sees the change in the flight angle. It's a ripple in the calm of the world, and she doesn't like it. Her head goes up, and goes stiff, and she brings up the heads of the other hinds like a puppeteer. Vicarious alarm isn't as intense as first-hand fear. In this friendly wind the other heads go down after a couple of minutes, but the old bitch isn't satisfied. She's looking straight at us. *Please, please, somebody: tell her that the ground breathes, too.* You look down, thinking that she can see us blinking, and then look back. She raises her head further, and her nostrils swell. Perhaps some of your scent has rebounded off the cliff and leaked down the slope. After an age her nostrils subside and her head comes down. She's grazing again, but she's shifted her position so that she's pointing at you.

You give her another five minutes and then pull yourself forward, about an inch a century. There's a nice calculation to make: the danger of moving faster and being seen has to be weighed against the danger of the wind changing. It only has to swing ten degrees, or rattle down the stream, and she'll have you, and you'll never get near that stag. A billiard ball coming off a green cushion is unpredictable enough: the game now is about tumbling smell in a gusting tide of rocky bagatelle.

And no, that sentence doesn't make sense and I don't care: this is life and death, and if you don't mix metaphors you're not doing it properly. There are so many imponderables that you'll kill the stag only if God wants you to, and don't you dare think that would be a mark of favor.

Her head's up; her head's down; up, down. Whatever you do or don't do is irrelevant. If the stag's doomed, it's doomed. It's too late for prayers, for him and for you, and they don't work anyway in land like this. No: your actions aren't completely irrelevant; you can do something that hurts. That's the sort of currency that'll buy stuff out here. So you force your cheek against a rock until you can feel there's no skin left, and that does bring a kind of clarity, and, better, it keeps the bitch's head down. A hundred yards to the lump of grass where it's all going to happen. It will be good to be there, but you hope that she'll get your wind. Far better not to have a shot than to miss, and for sure you'll miss: your fingers are dead; and you're not good enough. By which you don't mean "good" in the sense of being a good shot, but "good" in the moral sense. Look at that thing: the size of its neck. It's always the neck. And then look at your white legs, exposed where the hill has pulled down your socks. You're pathetic, and to be pathetic means that you're undeserving. Thin white legs don't deserve to bring down that neck. They're thin and they're white because they haven't done anything heroic, and they haven't done anything heroic because they're thin and white, and the ethic out here, old boy, is Homeric or bloody nothing.

You're at the grass. This hasn't been unpleasant enough for a kill. There have been moments of enjoyment, and they'll make the bullet swerve. Up on your elbow. The rifle bolt's deafening. Everything between here and Inverness will have jumped at that. There's a glistening bullet crouched on the blocks. Better leave the safety catch on; there's a sprig of heather that could snatch the trigger. Up to the shoulder. The stag shifts. He's too end-on now. You might just clip his leg or chew up his guts. Gun down. It'd be hell if he lay down, and he just might. But the wind and stars have shifted and the bitch is now your friend. She's jumpy, and it's infectious. She's about to go. Her haunch sinks so that she can blast up and out. Even this suave, blasé stag takes notice. He twists around.

Because your skin and blood are on the stone back there, and that's apparently enough, and because there's mercifully no time, it's easy. To the shoulder; catch off; crosshairs up the front leg: as soon as you see chest, squeeze and keep squeezing. You squeeze the bullet all the way through the air into the left ventricle: it won't go unless you keep squeezing. Imagine yourself squatting in the stag's heart. Reel the bullet in. Or beckon it in, slowly and emphatically.

There's a thump and a stagger. It doesn't look like much, but the ventricle is mincemeat, and, bored with the heart, the bullet has gone off wandering. The stag coughs. It seems an inadequate response. This, after all, is the biggest thing that's ever happened to the stag. It warrants more than a prosaic, workaday cough.

The stag's off. That, too, is unworthy: there really is no point in running. It just has to be faced, and what better place to face it than right here, with a storm building over the sea and the raven angling back in for a beakful of bowel, and the five o'clock news just starting on the Land Rover radio? His horns, sticking out of the heather, are more trees than swords. There's a fly on his eye by the time you get there. "Nicely done," says the stalker, and if there's any decency in you you'll have no idea what he's talking about.

We don't go in for he-man snuff photos (me and a dead animal that's better than me except that it's dead and I'm strangely not). A knife that you never noticed before slides in, and the belly uncoils like fat hot snakes. They're still squirming as you head down for your bath, forgetting how it really was and translating the day into something that'll do for dinner chat.

By the time the gong goes the stag is dead and never really lived, and you, my friend, are an effective predator, splendidly lonely at the end of the food chain, perched in bright sunlight on the teetering summit of an ecological pyramid, and the Sophoclean's there, too, smiling and slow clapping.

* * *

There is another way to be a wolf. On Exmoor there is an ancient herd of around three thousand red deer, and there are staghounds to chase them.

I'd catch the train to Taunton on a Friday, spend an uneasy night wondering how I'd cope with a broken neck, get up in the early hours to meet a mountainous horse in a rainswept lay-by, and head off across the moor after a horn, too busy to be afraid.

Every other day, on average, the hounds would bring a stag to bay in a river, where it was shot. And every inch of the average twelve-mile run retaught me things I'd forgotten about how to be a human child. On the back of a horse I was as high above my usual height as I'd been below my current height as a six-year-old. The gorse and heather were tumescent and psychedelic with my surging serotonin. Everything was made new with every lurching stride in this epiphanic Wordsworthian bloodfest. The trembling horn from the valley bottom, always pubically, triangularly wooded: "*Whoooooooooo*. It's died. It's died. It's died." "So that we can live," came the echo from wet rock. It was all very complicated, this death and sex and childhood.

Sometime between then and now I began to have some idea of how time works; how long it takes for humans to change;

for habits to become ingrained; of the ratio between the intensity of experience and its apparent duration. On a train rattling back to Oxford I started to sketch out, on the back of a paper about the moral status of the embryo, some fanciful metaphysical calculus. Although a few red deer may reach the age of twenty, fifteen years is a good old age. Say that fifteen deer years are equivalent to eighty human years. One deer year, then, is 5.33 human years. Say, too, and conservatively, that a deer does five times as much living in its converted year per unit time as a human: that's five times as much attention to the world around it, and factoring in the relatively smaller amount of sleep that deer have. That means that . . . It was nonsense. I crumpled the paper and threw it away. I was left with the bare, unquantified conviction that red deer put me to shame, and that to be alive longer I should learn from them, get up earlier, and wander wood and heath by night—an amorphous but quite practical conclusion.

Since I'd concluded that red deer lived more intensely than I did, I should probably have been uneasier about my own predatorhood. I should have concluded that killing them was more morally serious than I thought. I didn't, because no one, and least of all me, is morally consistent, and because I was having too much fun.

* * *

I wasn't converted in a Damascus road moment as I watched a deer I'd shot spray blood from her nostrils onto the snow and try to reach her friends in the wood; or as I saw a hunted hind, with calf at heel, lift it up with her nose and dump it in a stand of bracken so the hounds wouldn't find it; or as I was asked to admire a photo of a beaming oaf from a bank kneeling beside a Highland royal that he'd wounded twice and that a contemptuous stalker had to finish off; or as I read about the men of Porlock standing by in their boats on hunting days to chase, lasso, and slit the throats of deer that swam out to sea; or as I drank old Burgundy at dinner in the lodge, trying and failing to feel heroic after a flukey lethal shot; or as I lay tucked up in goose down, watched by gilt-framed patriarchs in plus fours, listening to the rain that was lashing the back of the stag on the hill that I'd set out to kill after the morning kedgeree.

Those moments helped, but it was really politics that did it. The moments contributed to the politics, but not as much as they should have. I needed to see that humans were also victims in order to realize that there might be something wrong with animal victimhood. When I'd seen children ridden down by shareholders, or wounded and left to die by CEOs, and death creeping sneakily up the glen to within rifle shot of my own family, I was ready to make the connection. Until I became a bleeding heart leftie I couldn't write meaningfully about bleeding harts.

I continued, though, to think that being an effective predator helped me to know something about my prey species. That was very wrong.

* * *

Matt, a plasterer from Dunster, met me outside the White Horse in Stogumber. His family had chased foxes and hares across Exmoor and the Quantocks for generations, and in the back of his van were some of the country's best-nosed bloodhounds. One of them, Monty, was going to hunt me.

"Let him have a sniff of your boot," said Matt. "I bet we'll have you before you break a sweat."

I set off running along the side of a field of young maize. It had been raining, and there was now a hot fog rising from my footprints. It was bad weather for being a hunted deer.

I wasn't going to be killed, but still the chase seemed to matter very much. That's the neurotic temperament for you.

A piece of grit in my shoe, which I'd usually have ignored, was vast and malignant—conspiring with the universe for my destruction. The low, dry fences were high and slippery. I retched up my heart and it sat hunched in my throat, stopping the sea-fog-air from seeping into my blood. I was rushing, and, mockingly, nothing else was. The field was brutally, callously relaxed. A beetle crept calmly down a maize stem. I hated it for its leisure and indifference.

That was for the first few hundred yards, when the maize clutched my legs and the only rhythm was the tickling throb of my throat. Then I stumbled out of the field and could stride, and my heart retreated to my ribs, and again there was a tide in my chest. The wood was still maddeningly leisurely, but it wasn't out to get me. Everything seemed to have a voice, and now the voices were, by and large, sympathetic. The nettles apologized for stinging my legs and assured me that they'd do a far better job on Monty's drooping lips, which were swaying up toward me.

But then I began to doubt the kindness of the wood. A carrion crow, which by all the rules should have scrambled as I thrashed past it, sat and watched me from a branch five yards above my head. I saw myself in its eye: hunched and panting. I'd have thought that everything in a crow's eye would be black, but I was a brilliant red. I thought, absurdly, that it was waiting for me to be killed so that it could pick up some scraps. This was very undeerlike behavior.

In other ways, though—mostly unconscious—I was behaving very much like a hunted deer. My adrenals were pumping out cortisol and adrenaline. The cortisol made me taut. (The next day its immunosuppressive effect threw open the drawbridge of my throat to an invading virus.) Blood was diverted from my gut to my legs. Though I was slumping from the effort, I'd stop from time to time, hold my head up high, and reflexively sniff. If I'd had mobile ears they'd have pricked and swiveled. Though I looked for water, as deer do, to cool me and to send my scent spiraling away, I ran on the driest ground I could find. I knew (from well before birth, rather than because I'd read books and watched hounds) that dry earth doesn't hold scent well, or, if it holds it, hugs the particles close, leaving few for snuffling noses.

Unlike a deer, though, I longed to be out of the wood. It's often very difficult for staghounds to push deer into the open. Sometimes it takes hours. The deer double back, lie flat in deep cover, and saber-rattlingly confront hounds rather than breaking out.

It would have made sense for me to stay in the wood. Scent bounces off trees like balls in a pinball machine and eddies like the dark, curd-coated corners of the East Lyn River. It's hard for even the most educated nose to read it there. Out in the open, there's a slime trail of scent through the grass. It points in the direction of the prey. It's easy to extrapolate forward and back. Yes, the wind can knock the scent about, but it usually just shifts the trail a few yards downwind: the line will still be clear enough.

My preference for the open was therefore strange. I suppose we want to die where we've evolved, just as an overwhelming majority of people say that they'd prefer to die at home. We evolved on an East African plain. Like most people, I now express this inchoate preference in many neurotic ways: in a fear of the dark and of caves (though, like everyone else, I began life in a totally dark, pounding cave, and was safer there than I've ever been since); in a need to have the curtains open at night so that I can see turning stars and tell myself that the universe is still doing what it should; in the malaise I get in a room with no natural light; in the conviction that maggots eating something underground are more obscene than maggots eating something in the sunshine; in shuddering at coffins. A private hospice on a mountainside could charge a lot more than one in the suburbs. It's no surprise that seaside towns are full of retirees, desperate for a big view as the sun sinks. It's all because of Tanzania.

No: I wasn't going to die. But I couldn't tell that to my adrenals. They pushed me on through the maize. My breath was deafening. I couldn't hear anything else.

I hadn't expected silence. I'd expected an exhilarating duet between baying hounds and rasping lungs. That would have been an appropriate, dignifying, and comforting soundtrack to the drama. But there was no noise at all behind me: no deep funereal belling from between wobbling jowls.

This silence was hard to take. That, too, is a legacy from the savanna, and another reason for my suspicion of woods. Neurologically I'm set up to expect dangers, opportunities, and options to be pretty clear. I'm a long-distance viewer of zebra herds, shifting clouds, and waving grass. There are unseen, unheard, and unsmelled things on the plains, but they are calculable. There's a fair chance that there will be lions in that long grass: I'd better skirt it to get to the zebra. My skill is not in detecting the dangers: it is in mentally testing out the possible responses; it's in painless, risk-free optimization.

But, panting in that Somerset field, I didn't have the data necessary to start calculating. I am physiologically set up to avoid dying gloriously in the open, and thus have a distinct preference for dying in the open rather than elsewhere. My heroic metanarratives have evolved to justify my physiological settings. "How can man die better," asked Horatius, urging the Romans to hold the bridge against the surging Etruscans.

than facing fearful odds;
For the ashes of his fathers
And the temples of his gods?

That's the poetic corollary of being able to see zebras and have a pretty fair stab at anticipating lions. We are creatures with faces. We face things. We're good at it. And when we can't, we panic. We always panic when we can't do what we're good at, which is why office workers, who are naturally good at running down wounded kudu, are stressed to hell, fearful, and overmedicated.

There was no hound for me to face, and that scared me. Adrenaline and cortisol didn't help much here. In fact they were a detriment, just as they are to hypertensive wage slaves. They steeled my muscles, but froze my mind.

I knew I hadn't won. These hounds are as inexorable as age. They can follow a scent that's twenty-four hours old. They don't hurry. They have faces so funny that they are well beyond a joke. They can't be conned or distracted. They work steadily down the ledger, calculating and double-checking. They're not excited by what they do, and so there's no hope of mistake, as there is with exuberant, blood-hungry foxhounds. Foxhounds get drunk on the scent and dribble with excitement. Bloodhounds dribble all the time, but with diligence. Foxhounds are the charismatic prosecutors; bloodhounds are the dull ones who've read and reread the brief. If I'm a guilty defendant, give me a flamboyant prosecutor every time.

Monty caught up with me on the side of another maize field. He was ten yards away when I first saw him. When he saw me, from under those heavy roller-blind lids, he just turned away. He didn't need any consummation other than a checkmark on his time sheet. The job was done. He turned around and ambled back up to Matt, who was several minutes behind.

The silence hadn't just been unnerving; it was hurtful. I ride a clanking bicycle around Oxford, and I have a prepared speech that I make to myself whenever people can't hear me approach and don't get out of the way. It goes something like this: "You're in my way. I'm a fast-moving frame of steel and fat, and I'm making a noise that, half a mile off, would have sent any of your ancestors onto their bellies, clutching their assegais and trying to stop their hearts bursting out of their chest. I'm a yard behind you: you've no idea I'm here. You've lost so, so much. I'm better than you. I'm going to recall you to the possibility of being alive by sounding this enormously powerful horn, thus . . ." I've got evangelistic about this. I go out of my way to cycle through the parts of Oxford grazed by huge placid herds of insensate tourists, hoping to summon them back to what they might have been.

Monty had managed to do exactly the same to me. He'd never have done it to a red deer. But I was glad to be comprehensively humiliated and scared. To be brought down with a *whoo-whoop* after a five-mile point on airy downland wouldn't have taught me about being prey. It would have been like a greyhound race—a contest between two predators—in which I'd come off the worst. Being prey is never glorious.

Usually large prey species are killed quickly. Those epic hunts of caribou by wolves for many hours make good TV, but they are unusual. Usually wolves explode out of the trees, course for a few hundred yards, and then either kill or give up. That's just how the thermodynamic arithmetic generally works.

Unlike wolves, staghounds don't give up. That's at the root of most reasoned opposition to stag hunting with hounds. Red deer, the argument goes, never evolved to be long-distance runners. They rarely had to be. They're sprinters. But hunted deer on Exmoor run for an average of around twelve miles, and for around three hours. That, it's said, is likely to exact a painful physiological price. If you've trained to run the hundred meters, it's going to hurt to run a half marathon. There's a loud, bitter debate about whether there is credible evidence of those physiological costs.

We can argue about what the high levels of lactate mean for the stag's subjective experience of suffering, or whether the burst red blood cells are artifactual. The physiological debate is important, but I'm not sure that it contributes much to the ethical debate. Of course there is a physiological cost to pursuit: the animal is brought to bay precisely because it runs out of the funds necessary for continued payment. The cost is plainly more than when a high-speed projectile smashes up the heart of a grazing stag. And the physiological toll must have some "emotional" corollaries. (You leave those quote marks in or out, as you please.) There's much more adrenaline surging through the hunted stag; its neurons are burning like the bars of an electric heater as the messages spurt through them. But whether that's painful is a matter of definition and opinion. The membrane between pain and pleasure is often thin and sometimes invisible. Pain brings pleasure: as the tiring stag leaps over a farm gate, tearing some muscle fibers, its brain gets a euphoric, analgesic dose of endogenous opioids.

I've run long distances: sometimes fifty miles at a time, and then up the next morning to run a lot more, carrying all I need on my back. The cacophonous scream of the muscles is orchestrated by a masterly Mozartian brain into harmonies that are lovely—lovely because they chime with the frequencies of the rest of the wild. When I've crept, cramped, bleeding, and blistered, into a sleeping bag, I've always said: "So this is what legs are for, and this is what being alive feels like!"

This might be because I'm a masochistic pervert, in which case it's unlikely to say much about hunted red deer. But that's not necessarily the case.

I'd rather be killed outside, after fifteen heart-bursting miles, having tried every possible ruse: having taken the hounds plunging through pad-ripping gorse, with my having been tried and found wanting, with a good chance achingly forfeited, with my natural heroin beginning to pry my consciousness out of my throbbing head, with a splendid malicious hope of disemboweling a hound, with a look, through salt-stung eyes, through the haze to Wales, than be chewing cud, and then a thud and the dark.

But perhaps that's just me. A quick, unreflective death (ideally, it seems, a catastrophic heart attack at dinner) is what everyone seems to want. It's a fashion. A few generations ago people prayed to be saved from sudden death: they prayed for time; for context; for goodbyes; for the chance to take stock and to make memorable gestures. Now the prayer is to be spared all this: to be catapulted without warning into the void. Very odd.

Red deer, though, don't have much idea about their own death. *Timor mortis* shouldn't be added to the indictment against the staghunters. Hunted deer are fearful, but you can have fear without having a clear reason to be afraid, and indeed there are many reasons other than the fear of personal extinction to be afraid of snapping teeth.

The rumpus, noise, and confinement of the slaughterhouse alarm cattle and sheep that are processing to their death, but they don't seem to be particularly distressed, or to make any obvious attempt at evasion, when a captive-bolt pistol or a gun is put to their head. They graze happily around the recently dead corpse of a flockmate or herdfellow. Horses behave entirely naturally in the presence of other, badly injured horses, even when there are major wounds, copious hemorrhage, and protruding bones. They'll have a sniff of a horse corpse in a field, then carry on eating. Sheep and pigs aren't obviously affected by witnessing the stunning and sticking of conspecifics. When farmed red deer are shot in a field, the others are slightly alarmed by the noise of the shot, but the sight of the cadavers themselves doesn't seem to move them until there's a sufficient number lying dead for the deer to perceive the gun (as opposed to the death that springs out of it) as a specific personal risk. They'll happily eat potatoes that have fallen out of the mouths of dead deer—unless they're visibly covered in blood. Red deer are programmed to avoid danger, but in their definition of danger there's no existential category, and so there's no existential angst.

Fearing one's own death and empathizing with the death of another aren't the same thing: presumably death row psychopaths don't go quietly into the night. But there's an obvious connection. If deer were horrified by the sight of a dead deer, we could *start* to argue that they subjectively fear their own extinction. The fact that they're not makes it hard even to begin the argument.

That's not to say that the deaths of other animals are emotionally irrelevant. Herbivores have relationships with one another that no doubt have some emotional color. To kill an animal that has been part of the survivor's life is to destroy an ecosystem. That's bound to disturb. But it seems that with ruminants, horses, and pigs, the disturbance is not triggered by outraged empathy. Indeed, there's little evidence that they're empathic at all. They're machines; islands; cold gene bearers.

Although there are methodological difficulties with many of the studies on animal empathy, there's significant evidence that some species are genuinely empathic. Rhesus macaques, rats, and pigeons may refrain from pressing a bar to obtain food for themselves if doing so causes another conspecific to receive an electric shock. In macaques the effect is stronger if the monkey doing the pressing is familiar with the victim, or if it has been shocked itself. And after a fight, chimpanzees (and possibly several other mammal and bird species) disproportionately console the recipients of violence (as opposed to the aggressors). Muttering "reciprocal altruism" or "kin selection" won't make the emotions associated with this behavior any the less real or intense.

If pigeons, rooks, and rats are empathetic, it's perhaps surprising that charismatic larger ruminants aren't. You'd expect something big, brown-eyed, and long-eyelashed, which spends a long time meticulously and sacrificially mothering a single calf, to do better. Perhaps it's because death is part of their constitution in a way that it's not for other species. They are made to be food. It's what they're *for* and what they *are*. Death isn't alien: it's not an invader that needs to be feared.

C. S. Lewis remarked that if the reductionists were right, humans should not complain as they do about death. They should breezily accept it as something as natural as breath. "Do fish complain of the sea for being wet?" he asked. That humans complain about death was an indication for him that they weren't designed to die. That red deer don't complain about death is an indication that they are.

Morality, at least in part, is about the fulfillment of natural expectations. It's less morally culpable to eat an herbivore than a carnivore. Herbivores expect it, and carnivores don't.

In every culture there's a taboo about eating carnivores. The shamans agree with Yahweh.

* * *

By being chased for a while, and by obsessing hypochondriacally about death, I hadn't undone decades of apprenticeship in predatorship, nor could I unravel the double helix. Yes, I have ancestral memories of narrow eyes just outside the reach of the fire, and fire itself makes me feel secure. You can buy a calming MP3 of the noise of a crackling fire. I'm happier where there's a tree with a low branch that I can reach but wolves can't. I feel that it's important, not just entertaining, to read "Little Red Riding Hood" to the children. Death itself is a maw, with, sometimes, a wiggling uvula. I have a thirst for physical integrity, and a curiosity about amputation, that can be explained only by a subliminal fear of death by rending.

Yet these are only punctuation marks in my story, not defining adjectives. The story itself is about me striding out from the fire, brand and spear in hand, and the eyes scattering. The wolf in Grandma's bonnet is a victim. I always get to the low branch and taunt from there before throwing the lance. I'm kept warm in my own Ice Age by the skins of speared wolves. I'm the predator of predators: I eat steak without becoming steak.

Only the cold turns me into a deer. We grew up in it together, some time in the Pleistocene.

* * *

In the winter, deer come down from the tops. They were near the track across Rannoch Moor from Inveroran: heads down, even when I was close, a few of them raking the snow with sharp feet, using each other as wind baffles; most of them still. Their heavy coats couldn't hide the tucked-up bellies. Snow had been lying here for a couple of mean months. There was grass there if they scraped hard enough: August sun freeze-dried. But it was touch and go whether it was worth it: the margins were tight, and the tentativeness of the feet showed it. Tentativeness like this is never far from death. Wilderness cooperates only with prudent confidence.

I took off my backpack and crawled toward them on my hands and knees. This wasn't an attempt at concealment: I was in full view. Nor was I trying to be a quadruped. It was just slightly more efficient than walking on my hind legs. Each step took me in above my waist. It was better to swim-burrow through the snow. I was more of a mole than a deer. I couldn't understand how the deer could stand just ankle deep, or how they could get to the grass. I didn't meet a blade of grass for two hundred yards in my trench. Then the ground climbed, and the snow fell away, and I knew that the deer were standing on a high plateau, and that the wind had swept it clean for them.

They saw that I was an unarmed torso with useless, flailing, bloodless limbs. They had a bovine vacancy I'd not seen before in deer—even in fat, farmed, unstimulated deer. I had their sour wind. I took it in my throat, not my nose. There was something else on my nose: pear drops—the ketones of starvation. These deer were burning their muscle and were going to die. If the stalker dropped hay all around them they'd stand and look at it and then lie down and be eaten. By the time it gets to this point it's a kind enough way to go. You go to sleep and are blown away and what's left freezes to the ground and is then carried up to the crag on black wings.

I sat there among them for hours. By the end of that time there was no more scraping. They were all dead still, like monuments to themselves. They barely turned their heads when I burrowed back to the path.

I'd been stupid. I was wet through. I'd been warmed by solidarity with the deer, but now there was danger. There wasn't much light left. I'd struggled a long way up from the road running through Glencoe, and now there were feathers of snow in my face. A black figure rose out of Loch Linnhe. It straightened up over Kinlochleven, then leaned over Glencoe and opened its mouth, and out of its mouth stooped a fat flapping bird of a snowstorm that skimmed low over the Kingshouse, spread its wings wide over Rannoch, and landed with its claws out. The claws didn't get me, but the wings clipped my face, blinded me, and pushed me to my knees.

I got up, and went down, and got up and went down and got up and went down. And after a while I didn't care much. The snow punched me; the cold bled me. It was very interesting. Then I got too tired to be interested. I badly wanted to go to sleep, mainly because sleep meant blankets and coziness. I wanted to pull something over me, and I didn't really mind if that was snow. With a blanket over me the noise would stop: the growl rolling in from the sea.

Then a thin, clear, pedantic, ascetic voice, which I recognized as mine, said something like: "You'd better get out of the wind." And I replied: "Ah, to stop the growl, and be warm?" And I replied to it: "Well, yes, if you want to see it that way." And then I added, seeing that some advocacy was called for: "If you don't, you see, you'll not have beans on toast again." "Ever," I added, histrionically, in the pause that followed.

So I, or we both, found a bit of a wood and a bit of a wall, and we took out a sweater and another hat and one of those big thick plastic survival bags that you never use, and through the night we worked our fingers and toes and added up and tried to factorize all the phone numbers we could remember, until there was a kind of dawn with no growl in it, and on each side of us, against the wall, were red deer that didn't stink of pear drops and yet looked at us like kind old dogs.

* * *

I couldn't eat what the red deer eat. Wherever the deer are, half or more of their diet is grass; then (at least on Exmoor) come ericaceous shrubs and herbs, and then the leaves of broad-leaved trees—all with an occasional garnish of lichens and mosses and the odd coniferous leaf. But I knew well every plant that the deer like. I'd smelled them and pureed them and made soup from them and pulled them up with my teeth and chewed them and then tried to vomit them up so that I'd have the taste of a cudding (not a successful or popular activity). Indeed, I'd tried generally to belch more—to live with my food for longer; to revisit repeatedly, and well into the night, the lunchtime fish fingers and chips.

In a little book I had lists of adjectives for chewed

bramble, ivy, nettles, sorrel, and many species of moorland grass. I had similar lists of adjectives for other parts of a deer's world that I'd aped: what it's like to defecate into the north wind; what it's like to be woken by a jay; how a dead calf smells in the sun, and how in the rain.

I let my hair grow shaggy and coated it with mud. I noted how long the smell of my own urine lasted on peat, on stone, and in broad-leaved woodland in various climatic conditions. I speculated about the reasons for red deer's distaste for coniferous woodland, why hinds spend a much higher proportion of the night than the day in deciduous woodland and why it's the other way around with stags, and I lived the patterns of both for several nights and several days in several seasons.

I made parallels between athlete's foot and foot rot and, to learn the feel of overgrown hoofs, didn't cut my toenails for months.

I said to myself: I can scan my olfactory inputs, as a CT scanner takes slices of an object, and examine each slice for traces of anything I want; there's no need to take the scent of the valley as a whole. You'd never say to a waiter "I'd like to order the menu, please." Only human noses would do that. Slowly, slowly, I began to have an à la carte nose.

It might seem sensible to set out the results of all these games. But I won't. I came to see them as pointless.

* * *

Meeting with the deer in the cold—when we were both on the cusp of annihilation—was one thing. But then we were hardly ourselves. Whatever we were was so lean and strung out that it didn't have the shape of a striding human or a leaping deer. To meet deer there wasn't really to meet deer at all: it was to meet wraiths. It's not true that extremity shows us our true colors. Those are seen in times of plenty. What matters—what makes us—is how we handle wealth.

The deer wait, patiently or impatiently, for plenty. It comes in the summer. If they're to be known, that's the time to know them, and that's the time when they're hardest to know.

In the heat, Exmoor deer are often buried antler deep and deeper in the ravines, the wood winding all around and over them, columns marching along their brow tines, fly clouds like a humming perm around their dung. The deer lie still, listening for grass being parted and crushed rather than stirred, chopping up the scents, grading them in order of seriousness, and attending to them strictly in that order.

On a day in mid-July, just after dawn, I climbed into the steep side of an old oak wood and slid down with the sticks to the valley bottom, where there were a few yards of tangled respite from the hegemony of gradient.

From above and far away the wood looks like moss. From inside it looks the way that moss looks to a weevil. Sometimes there's a suggestion that a branch has moved, far off, against the grain of the breeze. But it is never more than a rumor. You never get more than a rumor of red deer in the high summer woods.

They'd been here. Yet the fact that they'd been here made them seem less accessible than if there were no sharp slot among the wood vetch. The slot meant absence, as the belongings of a dead parent mean absence. If the belongings hadn't been left, there would always be the possibility that the person might reappear. It's the artifacts that make it impossible to deny the loss.

There's a pool here, the shape of a twisted lip. Bracken leans over it, and bracken leans over the bracken, except where a red stag has lumbered up and out, taking a snagged slipstream of fronds on his head. This green cap on the pool pens in the stag scent. The scent is gently stirred, but not diluted, by air seeping down from the moor. There are thick, crisscrossing stag hairs on the water surface. The pool looks like a shattered window or a psychotic dream of ten thousand telescopic rifle sights.

I undressed and slipped into the pool. I went down to my thighs in the mud, threw myself back in alarm, wrenched my legs slowly out, and lay panting on my back, trying to keep my body submerged and out of reach of blood-lapping horseflies.

The pool was a nursery. Larvae whipped, floundered, and, losing their hold on the tense two-dimensional tightrope of the water surface, fell to the mud, which was made of other bodies. The water was frantic with dying things that hadn't been born. They matted on my skin. When a stag leaves the pool the sun dries all these animals on his coat. When you see him on the hill, you see the red hair through a seamless lens of dead invertebrates.

I lay until the alarm calls in the trees turned to territorial business as usual, which was when the mud had settled on my chest. Then I came primordially out, my limbs about as effective as a coelacanth's fins, and curled naked in the bracken, trying to conjure danger and fear in place of the feeling that this was interesting and colorful.

I couldn't do it. But I could be watchful, which is how the stag would be with its danger and fear. I could map the bird territories, so that I could plot the metastasis of alarm. I could chart the wind, and face away from it so that my eyes could cover the ground that my nose would not. I could recalibrate my visual sensitivity to movement, so that I'd freeze when a branch swung in a new arc. And, like a diligent veterinary student, I could become very familiar with the normal so that I'd know the abnormal. So I learned the skyline, photographing it in my head and then closing my eyes and trying to recall every bump. I learned the voices and temperaments of the farm dogs above and behind me.

I badly wanted to get dressed. My mud and chitin coat helped, but the flies were thirsty. I cupped my scrotum like a footballer facing a thunderous kick. But I'd rationalized my pants back on too often. I soaked all my clothes in the pool so that they wouldn't be inviting, and went off to explore the wood.

I could do this at my own natural head height. An adult stag stands about fifty inches high at the shoulder, and from that shoulder height there are probably another couple of vertical feet to eye level. At my own eye level they'd taken desultory bites from the bracken (never a favored food) along their paths. They saw what I saw, though with red-green color blindness (draining the summer wood of some of its definition and variegation) but a sensitivity to ultraviolet light (blocked by robust filters in our eyes) that must make the flat blue sky, when it's visible through the swaying oak, swirl and crash like an angry Turner.

The challenge was to translate the wood not from deer-sense to man-sense, but from man-time to deer-time. This is the pace of growing, swaying, creeping things and then, in the space of a snarl, a bound from crouch to 40 mph. The head and the rest of the body must feel as if they're involved in two different road traffic accidents. The drag from the antlers must pull the head savagely back as the head and the body disconnectedly accelerate out of the furze.

I wallowed slowly in light, dew, and mud, trying to let the slow throb of the wood, rather than my own fibrillation, push the blood around my imagination. I raised my head at the speed of the sun. I tried to remember that the basic unit of time is a solar day, and that anything smaller is as artificial as Diet Pepsi.

For six hours I watched a single stem of robin-run-the-hedge move. Nothing around it moved. There was no vole tunneling beneath it or fanning bird above. It steadfastly waved.

The other stems steadfastly did not. Then it stopped. Abruptly. It didn't gradually wind down. The sun dried up the birdsong.

I moved to a patch of sorrel. The flies liked it less. From here, for another eight hours, I watched a spider bridge a gap between a baby beech and a baby oak. When the evening dew came, I saw that I'd missed almost all the web. An ant tried to crawl up my urethra. It seemed a compliment.

There's a time, just after dark, when the wood both clutches tightly to itself the last few shards of sunlight, seeming to arch over to keep them from running back, and exhales some of the sun it's soaked up in the day. This is the warmest time for a naked man, happily cushioned on sun and with sun thrown over him.

But the stars are pitiless. I pulled on my drenched clothes and walked back to the house.

* * *

Later that summer I lay in the middle of a gorse stockade on the top of our hill. The flowers were so yellow that they scorched the view, burning up all other color. The smell was an incongruous coconut.

"Give me five minutes," I'd said to the children. "Then come and find me and kill me."

"We will," they said.

It took them ten minutes to make the predictable mistakes: to look in the places that were obvious because they were not obvious; and then in the places that were obvious because they were obvious. Then they had to think.

"He's trying to be a deer," I heard one of them say. "He'll have gone to the water." So they searched the stream.

"He'll be under the trees," said Tom. "I heard him say that deer are really from the woods." So they looked under the trees. Then they got bored and went home to destroy something.

They didn't think of the gorse, because they didn't think

I'd need physical protection. Deer these days don't. Gorse is useful because, unlike bracken, it reduces to an easily monitored few the number of lines along which a wolf can oil or dash.

But there are no wolves. There haven't been since the fourteenth century, which is, for that reason, when modernity began.

These red deer spend a lot of their lives in ghost forests, whose trees were long ago felled for ships and sheep. They see the ghosts as solid: they duck to avoid entangling their antlers in branches that were lopped before Agincourt; they graze in the shadow of oaks that have cast no shadow since the Bronze Age. They can never exorcise the land. If they did, they'd exorcise themselves.

In this at least I can follow them. In fact I can't help it. No human can, although most modern humans—brutally exiled from the present by their neurology as red deer are by theirs—live in a phantasmal future rather than the past. But for me, a walk in the woods, or through a mall, is a séance. On a good day I'll spend about an hour being where I am, when I am. All of that hour demands either intense attention (when I'll bellow at myself, without much conviction: "I am *here*! *This* is *it*!") or children. For the rest of the time I look at a farm and smell woad bubbling, hear swords clashing, and see gray wolves bringing down red deer.

* * *

In his lyrical monograph *Red Deer,* Richard Jefferies says this about Exmoor: "On Haddon Hill the glance passes from Dunkery, which overlooks the Severn Sea, to Sidmouth Gap by St. George's Channel, so that the eye sees across the entire breadth of England there."

Red deer have good eyesight. There's no reason why they shouldn't see the breadth of England. So this was going to be a study of big sweeps; of context; of how an animal could be regional, and hence representative. I was going to swing for miles across the moor, fix my eye, seamanlike, on the misty blue horizon, sleep in ditches and drink spring water from Parracombe to Dulverton, hear the dialects of many hedges, write about geology, and come over all macroeconomic. It was going to be great.

But it was all ruined by the radio tracking data. No two fixes for any one animal were separated by more than 5.7 miles for stags or 4.2 miles for hinds. "Average range sizes within any one month or season," wrote the zoologist Jochen Langbein, dispiritingly, "suggest that red deer [on Exmoor] remain within fairly small areas spanning less than 2.5 miles for the majority of their time." Mature hinds range over around 1,000 acres. Adult stags do more traveling: they have (as I used to have) two distinct core ranges—one used mostly during the rut, and the other for the rest of the year—and the total territory is just under 2,500 acres. They do more traveling during the rut—just as I did. But the rut and the non-rut ranges only 1.2–3.5 miles apart: eerily close, in fact, to the distance between mine, now that I recall those taxi rides between Bethnal Green and Fulham. In my species and theirs the males tend to do the traveling.

It's not that these West Country deer are unusually parochial. Scottish Highland hinds have home ranges of about 1,000–2,500 acres, their stags 2,500–7,500 acres—bigger than those on Exmoor, yes, but only just, and only because the pickings on those bleak hills are much leaner. In the rest of Europe, seasonal shifts in range are small—rarely more than 6.2 miles—and are often nothing more ambitious than a winter shift downhill to keep out of the cold.

These are not regional creatures after all, and there was to be no big picture for me. Red deer would have to be yet another study in localism, and thus of locality. I'd wanted to walk long because to stay and to understand was too strenuous. If someone describes himself as a "traveler" on his website, as I do on mine, you can be sure he's on the run, and you should ask from what. In my case, I'm not telling.

These red deer well up from the ground. That might make it easier for them to go back into it. They are at home in a way that I cannot be. Human localness is uterine, not geographical. Humans cannot be properly at home once the uterus in which they grew up into relationship is burned or eaten.

* * *

Having lost the grand picture, I thought I'd make up for it with intensity. I'd understand five hundred hectares. From the map it should have been easy enough.

The red deer of Exmoor are moving fast up to the high moor—to Exmoor-Forest-that-isn't-a-forest—pushed from the gentler, wooded, more accessible fringes by the high price of venison. They're not made for the tops. The moors of Exmoor are a mountaintop that just happens to undulate on for miles, so that it looks like a moor. The deer have no fat on their backs, and don't have the temperament for a desert. There's peat under their hoofs here. They're walking on real paste from the trunks of the ghost trees they weave between. They may be safe from poachers' rifles, but they're more vulnerable to the hounds. The huntsman can see them a long way off, and if the hunted stag does a big loop, the hounds can be taken across the chord.

It's a hop and a skip from the cottage—up Brendon Common to the road, over the bridge where there are newts and trolls, and then off toward Hoar Oak Water—before you get to the parking lot with its pioneering brew-ups and rocking, grunting shag-vans from Wolverhampton.

In the spring I sat on the moor, waiting for the grass, and panicking when it didn't come.

In the summer I lay with the children in the woods and the bracken, watching streams of sugar coursing through plant veins bend aphids' snorkels. I pushed my own anarchic calves down when focused, unrambling ramblers marched past.

In the autumn I walked, rolled, and starved with the stags, but cheered quietly when I saw a wayward hind, bored with the strident bellow of eugenic prudence from the big stag, slipping off down the valley to spin the genetic wheel with the punier boy next door.

In the winter I sat, lay, and walked. Because the ground was hateful and made of dead stuff, I sat often in the branches of the trees I'd sat under in the summer. The deer endured, and I found again that I could meet them only in the shriveled place of our endurance.

And then I did it all again, and again, and again.

I was wearying of this. Back in the cottage I went in despair and disgust through the notebooks. They told me nothing about the world of a red deer, and too much about my own, which I was trying to escape. I was deep in the sickly waters of anthropomorphic whimsy, and sinking fast.

There was one overwhelming reason. However heavy their antlers, however royal their step, and however thick their necks, red deer are victims. Their landscape is the landscape of victims, invisible except through victims' eyes. Apart from a few minutes as I ran from Monty, a few hours as I shuddered among the deer in Glencoe, and a few poetical moments of imagined solidarity with cold hinds in Hoar Oak, I couldn't be a victim. Imagination and ingenuity could help me hunt down and see reflected in myself everything except perpetual, defining vulnerability.

That failure vitiated the inquiry. There was no point in not cutting my toenails if I couldn't also be persecuted from the beginning of time. I was stuck forever in the restaurant car of the Caledonian Sleeper, my rifle beside me and my targets all around me.

I couldn't reach the red deer on Exmoor or in Scotland. I'd have been nearer to them in a cardboard box in a shop doorway.

Clap, *clap*, *clap*, goes the Sophoclean, but now I'm not sure if he's being sarcastic.

6. SWIFT

Some humans think that they can write about swifts, dogs, and termites. Here are some reasons why they might think so, and some facts.

1. Some dogs know when their owners are coming home, even when the owner is hundreds of miles away, and when the owner has changed plans and is returning at a wholly unexpected time.
2. Some humans can do this, too. Kalahari bushmen know when a hunting party has killed, exactly what it has killed, and the exact time of return—all from fifty miles away. They used to assume that the white man's telegraph worked by telepathy.
3. A related phenomenon has its own name in Norway: *vardøger*. Someone hears footsteps, or the scrunching of a car on the gravel, or the opening of a door and the knocking of snow off boots. There's no one there. The person who's been heard will arrive in a few minutes. It's useful. There's time to make the tea or put on the posh frock.

4. Many of us can tell when we are being stared at.
5. Termites are blind. They communicate by scent and by knocking signals. The information that can be transferred this way is very limited. If a termite mound is damaged, and a scent- and noise-blocking baffle put in the breach, the termites on either side of the baffle can't communicate with each nother. And yet they repair the two sides so that they join perfectly. There's a master plan to which the individuals have access. Similar comments can be made about many of the activities of most social insects.
6. Flocks of birds, shoals of fish, and girls in a chorus line move together as part of a wave passing through the group. But the speed at which the wave passes is far faster than the reaction time of an individual. They're part of a superorganism, just as much as a honeybee.
7. Young cuckoos don't know their parents. Older cuckoos leave Europe for Africa about four weeks before the younger generation is ready to go. Young cuckoos find their way to the ancestral feeding grounds in Africa unaided and unaccompanied.
8. Monarch butterflies hatch in the Great Lakes area of the United States and migrate south to overwinter in the Mexican highlands. They migrate north in spring. But the first generation of migrants breeds in the southern part of the range (Texas to Florida) and then dies. It's their offspring who make it to the Great Lakes, where they breed for several generations. The generation that heads south for Mexico in the autumn is three to five generations away from any butterfly that made the trip south earlier.
9. Newly hatched chicks often get attached to the first thing they see. If that's a robot, they'll see that as their mother. In a famous set of experiments, a robot's movements were determined by a random number generator.

But the chicks who saw the robot as mother wanted it to be near them. They were separated from it by a barrier. And yet they could draw it nearer. They psychokinetically overrode the program. A control set of chicks, not imprinted with filial love for the robot, could not.

10. When a new compound is created (as happens a lot), it can often be very difficult to make it crystallize. It can take years. But if a group in, say, Cambridge manages to do it, a group in Melbourne will often do it the next week. The effect is well documented. Skeptics purport to explain it away on the basis that somehow the new crystal must have been carried to the other laboratory (the "chemist's beard hypothesis"), where it acted as a template for the crystallization. But usually no such connection can be demonstrated.

11. Similar effects are seen in animal behavior. If group X, in Oxford, manages after years to teach rats a particular trick, group Y, in Sydney, without any contact with the Oxford group, will suddenly succeed, too.

12. If you kill one of the two cells of a two-cell sea urchin embryo, a whole sea urchin (not half) develops. If you fuse two sea urchin embryos, you get one giant sea urchin.

13. A hand, composed of millions of individual cells of many different types, grows as far as it has to, and into the necessary shape. But no farther than it has to, and not into just any old shape.

14. I like some people. I dislike others, even when they have no definable, relevant faults. There are some kind, generous, sacrificial, entertaining people in whose company we simply can't flourish.

15. There are some places in which we can thrive and be happy and others, with apparently identical characteristics, where we cannot.

16. Love.

17. The Einstein-Podolsky-Rosen paradox: particles that come from a common source (such as two photons of light emitted from the same atom) remain somehow connected, so that what happens to one is instantaneously reflected in the other.
18. Sexual reproduction: a headache for neo-Darwinian orthodoxy because it hides and dilutes, rather than putting on center stage, genes that have been tested by natural selection and found to confer an advantage.
19. Although some diseases and trauma can ablate memory, no anatomical seat of memory has ever been identified in the human brain.
20. Altruism.
21. Community.

These are facts about swifts because they are facts about the world, and swifts are part of the world, as I am. The facts indicate that no qualification other than occupancy of a shared world is necessary for me to write about swifts. That is a great relief, because swifts are the ultimate other. I can write about them only because I'm other, too, or (depending on my mood) because nothing is other.

* * *

Sometimes they are not so far away. Just now, a few feet from my head, a swift has struck straight up—as straight as a plumb line, without braking or stalling—into the roof; as fast as thought, though bolder. If something is only as fast as thought, perhaps thought can keep pace. Yet thought cannot snatch the blueness of the height, or know that the whole life of each swift is a gasp.

This swift, which was bringing a ball of five hundred insects, bound with saliva, to bald nestlings in a hot vent in the eaves, screams down our street at the level of my upstairs study. It looks in at the making of books, people, and tea; on flowery duvets, Edwardian plasterwork, fake baronial paneling, rows of monographs on the glories of the Quattrocento; on bears, skulls, Tibetan masks, psychotic dolls, and a lot of polite desperation. It screams up and down for no reason except that it is good to scream, and because the day deserves it. It's not hunting for aphids, airborne beetles, or sex.

I can join it in the pointless scream.

* * *

This swift hatched in Oxford, four years ago. For six weeks it swelled like a boil. Then it toppled out toward our trash cans, found its wings before it hit the railings, roosted that night in the air, a couple of miles above Oxford, flapping occasionally into the wind and circling slowly up, and then, two weeks later, started on the journey to Africa.

It came back the following summer, circled our house, didn't breed, went again, again, and again to Africa, came back to Oxford, and then found a hole in the house and a home for its semen. Until it flew into our roof above my head it hadn't touched the ground, or a tree, or a building, or anything but insects and the air in four years.

* * *

There are two classes of words commonly applied to swifts: words about ethereality and violent words. They are not contradictory. The violence makes the ethereal accessible. Swifts lay open the sky so that we can go there. They slash the veil.

If the swifts didn't come, we'd be stuck with what we've got.

They were very late this year. I panicked. I'd get up very early, thinking that I'd heard a scream, and rush to the window. There was nothing there but pigeons as ponderous as I am: pigeons who sleep in trees and squat in the dirt.

And then, as I was lying on my back, they were suddenly there.

"Why are you crying, Daddy?" said Rachel, who was watching my face instead of the sky.

"Because it's all right," I said. "Because the world still works."

"Okay," she said.

They're always suddenly there or suddenly not there.

* * *

The air crawls. Up there, like plankton, there are live things drifting in the wind: aphids, other bugs, spiders, beetles. An aphid might be sucked from a grass stem in an English wood, up a gurgling plughole in the air, across the Pyrenees and the Strait of Gibraltar, and into the crop of a zitting cisticola at an oasis in Mauritania.

I've tried to map the vortices. It's best done from quite tall, bald trees with lots of footholds on which you can stand at many heights. It's a happy, mesmeric way to pass the day.

Airborne thistledown's the best marker of the vortices. Each seed probably doesn't weigh much more than an aphid.

Near the ground the thistledown is tentative. It moves from side to side, as if testing the worth of all the possible air channels. By four feet up it has decided where to go, though a fleck of down that started in the same flower head might well have chosen differently.

In a wood, or above a field, the vortices are an unseen forest of tangled chimneys. The chimney walls are quite hard. Not much escapes from them. They're often very close together, but they're rarely exactly parallel, and they sometimes even cross. Each has a tight centripetal glug, but they don't just channel straight up. Each has tides and eddies. Bugs and seeds bounce off one another and off the walls: they somersault and arabesque. An aphid that almost made it out beyond the canopy might be blown back down by the fat cheeks of the summer and pass one coming up that started its climb from the undergrowth an hour before.

At the top of the tree line there's a tangled delta. The chimneys swell, start to knot, and spill into a flat bowl that spins them together. The flotsam gathers pace; the streams are wider and denser.

The swifts graze the streams. Perhaps there's another delta and another flattening farther up. Certainly by an altitude of a hundred yards or so the pickings are thin. Yet swifts are often very much higher than this, where they're unlikely to be feeding.

It's different in open country. There the sun sucks up the earth hard. Banks of wind surf roll across the land, hit a wall, a ditch, or a ripple, and surge up, becoming mushrooms. The stalks of air are huge writhing rivers of tiny spiders and aphids, sometimes hundreds of yards wide, racing in tumbling spate from the fields to the high clouds. They rasp a hand plunged into them.

The summer sky is, usually, a rigidly stratified bird sandwich. The swifts feed at the top, the martins are below them, and swallows wobble the top of the grass with their wake. But the swifts sometimes slice down into the martins' patch, and when the sky is heavy with wet electric power, they're pushed farther down among the swallows to the fields and the lakes.

Swifts are selective, fastidious feeders. Although they catch five thousand or more insects a day, and though they have wide gapes like the mouth of a trawl net, they don't usually trawl. They go for the big, stingless insects. You can see them swing off their course to get them. And their discrimination is nuanced. When they hunt bees they take the stingless drones selectively. Try telling drones from workers at a speed of fifty feet a second. They're not just responding crudely to insect warning livery: they take plenty of stingless bee and wasp mimics. We don't know how they tell the difference, but it must be visual.

They are raptors—aerial sight hounds—snapping like terriers, and so they have two foveas: a shallow monocular one and a deep magnifying one. This deep device probably gives them some binocular vision, used for computing the distance of speedy insects. They're like cheetahs or peregrines. When a swift first spots a likely kill, it'll be at a similar distance from it, relative to the size of the prey, as a peregrine would be from a pigeon, a cheetah from a Thomson's gazelle, or I from a deer far across the hill. Identical visuospatial problems have to be solved in each case. Like a peregrine, the swift nods its head as it bears down, switching between devices—between the big picture and the detail. Both are needed for a efficient kill that won't leave a sting in the mouth.

Though they're mainly trophy hunters in the sky plains, swifts are not above a gulping, glutting feeding frenzy if the chimneys are serving up a fresh hatch.

I was once in the middle of one of these kill orgies. I was dragging a very small child along to day care to be contained for a while, when the air above a wood by the road exploded in black, screeching sparks. The swifts were among a new hatch rising from the treetops; not bothering with hairpin turns, just plowing through, jerking openmouthed heads from side to side to hit the areas of deepest density.

We ran across the road. I told the three-year-old to wait in the stinging nettles and scrambled up a tree as high as I could get. That was quite high. I swayed in a fork just below the top and pushed my head out into the killing zone of the delta.

I saw a tongue, squat, gray, and dry; I saw myself, pinched and saucer-eyed. I felt the cool electric grace of a downstroke on my face. I snapped a mouthful of nymphs and spat them onto the roof of a brand-new Merc dropping off a child from a house three hundred yards away.

It was the closest I ever got.

But becoming a swift? I might as well try to be God.

* * *

I strapped myself into a harness and was tugged by a parachute into the sky. It taught me the taste of height—but the taste to a palate designed for six feet above the earth, not six thousand. It taught me about the roar of the wind, but the roar in flapping ears fixed on the sides of a big crude block of a head, forced under a gushing tap. It didn't teach me how the temperature changed as I climbed: my face was too flushed with fear and thought to notice, and the rest of my body was wrapped in wool and nylon.

Swifts feel the ground by the shape of the breath it exhales. They smell their way through the scent columns. They hunt in a reflected image of the earth—an image as dense and sticky as a caramel apple.

I looked down at woods and fields and saw woods and fields. For a swift, woods and fields are pizza delivery joints. You never go to one of those. You just call and speak to a disembodied voice. You don't really have much of a picture of what's there. You've never thought about it. You probably know vaguely where it is. If pressed, you might use its location as part of a set of directions to somewhere else (as a swift may use some terrestrial signposts for navigation). But it has no intrinsic interest other than as the source of your pizza. The swift stays at home in the air, and the earth delivers.

It's not surprising that poets get all ethereal about swifts. If anything can be literally ethereal, swifts are.

The main problem with turning myself into a swift, though, isn't that it's an air thing and I'm a soil thing. It's speed. I'm a terribly slow animal. The difference between our relative perceptions of the texture of the air is vast, but it's as nothing compared to the difference in pace of our lives.

In terms of longevity, a swift is comparable to many humans. Swifts have been known to live to twenty-one. It's the amount of living that they put into each of the years that's the real difference.

Some arithmetic, because there is a type of truth in figures.

Each spring and each autumn they travel around 5,592 miles between Oxford and the Congo: that's 11,185 miles every year—which doesn't begin to account for the flying that they do in their ordinary lives. That's spread over about 66 days in the autumn (30 days of traveling, 36 days of stopover) and 26 days in the spring (21 days of traveling and 5 days of stopover).* In autumn they average around 186 miles per day toward the 5,592 miles, and in the spring 266 miles per day. Let's assume that on the migration stopovers they do 47 miles a day feeding, soaring, sleeping, and exulting. Let's say that in the rest of their lives they're doing 62 miles a day.

Thus:

Spring migration: 5,592 miles + 235 miles on stopovers
Autumn migration: 5,592 miles + 1,692 miles on stopovers
Remainder of year: 273 days @ 62 miles per day = 16,926 miles
Total for year: 30,037 miles

For 21 years that's 630,777 miles—about 1/150th the distance between the earth and the sun and 2.6 times the distance between the earth and the moon.

Swifts are about 6.5 inches long. I'm about six feet, three

---

* Estimated from data on swifts that breed in Sweden, whose migration figures are: for autumn, a mean duration of 69 days (30–99 days): 30 days of traveling and 39 days of stopover; for spring, a mean duration of 29 days (18–34 days): 21 days of traveling and 8 days of stopover.

inches tall—about 11 times the length. If I were to walk proportionately as far in 21 years, I'd have walked almost 1/13 of the way to the sun, or 29 times to the moon and back. If I kept up the same pace and lived to 84—a realistic equivalent for that long-lived swift—I'd have walked a third of the way to the sun and 116 times to the moon.

But it's not all traveling and killing (though think of the millions of individual, assessed, intimately targeted head turns and snaps there will have been). That twenty-one-year-old may have bred nineteen times. The average number of nestlings might be as high as 1.7 per season. That's 32 in its breeding lifetime. Multiply that by four for me: 128.

That's what they do with their time. But what about their perception of what they're doing? If (and yes, it's a big if) they're watching, as we do, a film of their own lives, how fast is it moving? And how frantic are those snapping heads?

If those questions mean anything at all, they must relate in some way, however crudely, to the speed of perception.

Snails move very, very slowly. Only if events are more than a quarter of a second apart will a snail perceive them as distinct. If you wave your finger in front of a snail four times or more a second, it will see a single, stationary finger. Sloth freezes movement: it blurs, simplifies, and integrates, and in integrating it loses a lot of the whole. It obscures the distinct parts of things, if time is an element of those parts, and concocts the lie that it sees things as they really are. It drains time out of our vision. Oversimplification is deceit.

Whereas speed, if you're up to it, can tell you the value of time; can let you see your business with the due contribution from time's perspective; can inject complexity and nuance. If, like many birds, you can hear sounds separated by less than two millionths of a second, you'll know the baroque complexity of apparently bland birdsong. If you're a human hearing that, you'll fall on your knees. Wonder is a function of the degree of resolution—in birdsong, in optics, in philosophy, in theology. Only those blind to the velvet flow of a caterpillar's legs and deaf to the grunt of a crocus as it noses out of the earth don't worship, and often they can't be blamed.

Another way of putting this is that really fast hardware and software can effectively slow down the world. The acutely discriminating bird hears what I'd hear if I turned the speed of the birdsong right down. I can probably hear two sounds as distinct if they're around two hundredths of a second apart. The bird's getting in one second what it would take me about two and three quarters of an hour to hear.

If the rest of the bird's tape runs at a similar rate, and the bird (let's call it a swift) lives for twenty-one years, then, since it has done ten thousand times as much living per unit time as I have, it will die at a real age of 210,000 years—the distance separating us from the time when the first modern humans evolved in East Africa.

Now let's try this with physical speed—which of course entails a lot of attention in many different neurological modalities. The snail can get by as a woefully crude visual discriminator because it moves over ground at a top speed of about a yard an hour.

The highest migration speed recorded for swifts over a long distance is (a plainly wind-assisted) 404 miles per day. The average for the spring migration is 209 miles per day. Measured by tracking radar, the flight speed of swifts on spring migration was 35 feet per second, which, if maintained over twenty-four hours, would be 569 miles per day. The fastest human runner, Usain Bolt, clocked 41 feet per second over 328 feet (100 meters). Then he stopped, panted, was wrapped in a blanket, handed an energy drink, and carried shoulder-high around the stadium. The swifts continue, 3,360 times farther per day, for the best part of a month, catching their own food and navigating across deserts, seas, and mountains. We, at our very best, are snails.

Of course there are obvious objections to all these nerdishly arithmetical types of comparison. I've been making them myself as I've tapped away. I agree with them all. But even if the comparisons are wholly worthless, it's worth making them to demonstrate their worthlessness, and so clear the ground for something else.

The figures might be the grammar of swifts. Grammar is necessary but not sufficient for poetry.

I've tried to be prosaic, because when it comes to swifts all poetry fails.

* * *

I can't follow the swifts into the air. I'm less like them there than when I'm on the ground. Planes, of course, aren't about the air at all. You're farthest from swifts in a hurtling tube full of flatus. The view's disembodiedly cartographical.

The air, for me, is necessarily about buckles and ball-crunching harness. I lurch, swing, and churn. At best I'm a huge aphid—a drifting piece of swift food. At least on the ground I can dodge and roll for whole seconds at a time, and on a mountain in a gale I can feel secure when wind is blowing around me at the same speed as around the head of a migrating swift. When I stripped off my clothes at the top of our moor I got feedback from my ruffled body hair that was not all that unlike the tingling from the touch receptors of the swift's filoplumes—minute, hairlike feathers that lie alongside the contour feathers, moving with them and letting mission control know where each of the big plumes is in space.

Water's better, I suppose, but still remote. There I'm as buoyant as the swift when it's sleeping two miles above the sea. My legs could be its forked tail: they do the same job. I can angle my arms like its saber wings, and they take me down or up. But the water takes away almost as much swift life as it gives. It takes away speed, and therefore swift time. A slow swift is perhaps even less of a swift than a stiff swift.

I'm best at being a swift when I'm on the ground. At least then I can see and smell the source of the air rivers the swifts are fishing, hear the thrum next to my ear of the wasp that will be broken three hundred yards up, and slap a fly on my arm at more or less the same speed as the swift's stubby neck would turn and its mandibles close on it.

* * *

Sitting on a bench in my Oxford garden, I followed the swifts with my eyes, despairing as they climbed up to roost in the air, beyond all eyesight, beyond all sense, sensibility, and words.

When they left I couldn't bear it. I followed them across the Channel and across France, noting down slavishly—like a bereaved disciple looking for relics or holy places—the things that the swifts might have seen or smelled or heard as they came this way. It seemed to matter that the smell of a Picardy bonfire was rendered properly in the notebooks: the birds might have caught beetles that the fire hoisted into a cloud. The chatter in a Pyrenean café was relevant: the same phrases were likely to have been used a fortnight before, at the same volumes, and at the same tables, and so to have ricocheted off the same mildewed whitewash and up into the air over the mountain at the same angles, contributing to the same hum and throb that the swifts knew, and giving a floating aphid the same sort of jerk that caused a swift's head to turn. The wine that night in an Andalusian courtyard had to be described exactly because nitrate from swift dung might have coursed into the grapes, and because insects that fed on the vines might have spiraled up in a fog of lemons and rotting shrimp and been taken by you know what. Or you know *who*.

The world was a web, fine as gauze, woven of causes—each cause connected to the others, and each traceable ultimately, if you followed things carefully, to the swifts. I suppose I was a gnat's breath away from psychosis.

It wasn't good. The swifts were alpha and omega, and that denigrated the rest of the alphabet and truncated my vocabulary. I obsessed like this for years. Sometimes it was an exhilarating game, which in my more pompous moments I dignified as a thought experiment: "How do swifts connect my tennis elbow with the collapse of an Icelandic bank?" I'd ask myself. In the few blessed moments of self-mockery I reminded myself of the story about the fundamentalist Sunday school.

> Teacher: Caleb, what's small, furry, eats nuts, has a long bushy tail, and leaps from branch to branch?
>
> Caleb: Well, I know the answer must be "Jesus," because it always is, but it certainly sounds like a squirrel.
>
> In my case the ultimate answer was always "swifts."

Then, overlying and consolidating this primary pathology, there was a second generation of weirdness. Just as pilgrims revere the footsteps of the disciples who revered the footsteps of the master, so I followed in my own swift-following footsteps. In the spring I'd sit watching the Strait of Gibraltar in the same bar, in the same seat, drinking the same sherry, because that's where I'd been and that's what I'd been drinking when *they* first made landfall. I'd ask the musicians to play the same tunes that had brought them in before. At the very end of April and the start of May in Oxford I'd keep my eyes fixed on the ground until I got to the end of the road where I always see them for the first time—fearful of seeing them elsewhere.

This sounds like (at least) severe personality disorder or OCD. Well, perhaps. But a kinder word is *habit*.

I'm happier with that. Indeed I'm excited about that. Habit might be a way into the swifts. All other portals seem to be locked and double-bolted.

Although they often seem to refute it, swifts are subject to the same laws of nature as I am. However strongly they taste of immortality, they die. Gravity doesn't mean as much to them as to me, but they're not immune to it. We share a jurisdiction, and hence a passport. We can live together; we can travel together; we already have some shared habits, and we can work on acquiring more.

"Laws of nature," according to the biologist Rupert Sheldrake (who collated many of the facts at the start of this chapter), are like habits. They tend to be true because that's the way the universe has become accustomed to behaving. Sodium and chlorine atoms naturally adopt the configuration that they do in the structure of salt crystals because they're used to it; it's been done trillions of times before; the template's established; the electrostatic grooves are nicely chamfered; things slide neatly together because practice makes perfect; habit is the line of least resistance; and habits have evolved because they work, and are maintained because they keep working.

As anyone's who's just taken up running or dieting will know, new habits are hard to develop. The universe is a hard surface on which to engrave new patterns. But once something's been done once, it's a great deal easier to do it again. Think of the chemist's beard and the rats in Oxford and Sydney. Once it's been done a thousand times it'll be easier still. No wonder the history of evolution so often looks jerky: nothing for many millions of years, and then a huge stride.

My fingers stopped growing because their tips hit the boundary of a remembered pattern. That was habitual behavior. It's what fingers do: they obey that pattern. The young cuckoos were drawn to Africa by a memory, ingrained into the cuckoos' collective unconscious, of what cuckoos habitually do. Jung got it right for cuckoos, fingers, and salt crystals.

This entails a lot of mystical talking. Sodium has to talk to chlorine; embryonic fingers have to talk to some sort of ideal finger; young cuckoos have to talk to their dead ancestors. The whole massive enterprise of migration becomes one vast Ouija board. It's creepy and Platonic. Swifts are tugged at almost twenty thousand feet by an impalpable tide generated by millions of dead swifts. They're corralled by dead sky-shepherds across the Pyrenees, the Mediterranean, the western edge of the Sahara, and into the Congo.

"You don't need to invoke any of that stuff to explain migration," said a well-known zoologist. "Orthodox biology does the job perfectly well. The birds have a genetic map. That tells them roughly where to go. Then there are all sorts of mechanisms that could fine-tune the process. Magnetite crystals in the head, perhaps. Internal clocks and the position of the sun by day; using cloud-penetrating UV light if they have to."

Really? Is it so easy? It was this conversation, more than anything else, that propelled me into Sheldrake's arms. Terence McKenna sprang to mind. "Modern science is based on the principle: Give us one free miracle and we'll explain the rest," he said. That comment was in the context of explaining the natural world as a whole. He went on: "The one free miracle is the appearance of all the mass and energy in the universe and all the laws that govern it in a single instant from nothing." Similarly with all the uncomfortable facts in the opening list. Give us the laws governing the tendency of genetically identical cells to conform to an invisible blueprint, and a mechanism for encoding the tendency and enabling the conformation, and we'll write papers describing what happens, using terms like "predetermined somatic differentiation" to try to conceal the fact that we don't have the first idea how it's done. Instill in young cuckoos a desire to go several thousand miles, without a guide, to the places in Africa where they'll bump into their genetic parents, and we'll speculate intelligently about how, once they've been there once, they might use magnetite to chart a more nuanced route back. Is a "genetic map" any less mysterious than the collective unconscious? Isn't a genetic map, indeed, just one small manifestation of the collective unconscious? But without the explanatory power.

You might doubt the explanatory power of Sheldrake's hypothesis, or question his empirical underpinnings, but he's doing science a lot more satisfactorily than someone who doesn't see that there's a problem with cuckoo migration that demands an answer more fundamental than an internal compass.

Sheldrake gives the name *morphic fields* to the forces that tug swifts and cuckoos in migratory tides, and finger cells thus far and no farther, and makes atoms lie obediently in a customary lattice. The strength of a field, he postulates, is partly a function of alikeness. Theoretically, I suppose, everything in the universe is bound together by some sort of field, but family resemblance increases the strength of the field.

This is really another way of talking about habit. Swifts share habits with swifts. Habits entrench habits, which in turn entrench habits. But we don't share habits just with other members of our own species: we share them with all other cohabitants. We become like our dogs and our dogs like us. If we live in a wood we acquire the accents of the trees.

It should be obvious that we don't learn just from things

that are biologically alive—whatever that means. Learning anything from anything is a clairvoyant exercise. I got my Greek from a live man who got it from lots of dead ones. And my teacher mediated it to me using genetic bequests that, for all I know, he got from Goths and Berbers. Certainly he, like me, shares much of his genetic coding with dead chimps, lemurs, newts, and fruit flies.

* * *

All this was exciting and promising, for I had some swift habits. Expensive, long-standing, deeply ingrained ones that took me on trains, boats, planes, and paths to pubs, gardens, old girlfriends' sofas, lighthouses, park benches, the edges of places, insurance company towers in Tel Aviv dressed in mirror glass, a primary school in Berlin, and dusty corridors beneath suburban eaves, full of bat shit and fiberglass.

I shared some swift habits and habitats already. And I had the desire to be one. Surely intention counts for something in the mathematics of morphic resonance?

* * *

There's a gay Lebanese hairdresser in a thumping West African town. His salon is a temple where he worships a gently demanding goddess. He would call her Beauty. Others would call her Kitsch, and they would be wrong. He's brought here everything he thought was best from the nations through which he's wandered. From Paris there are curtains so flimsy that a determined mosquito could head-butt through them. From Italy there are mosaics in distressed high-density polyethylene. But he had chosen to stay in West Africa, and the things he thought best from there were gravid mother goddesses, which crouched beneath the jacaranda with their hands on their bellies and antelope horns springing out of their foreheads, frowning eyelessly, their breasts always distractingly asymmetric.

I was in his courtyard with my pal Nigel, who sells Iron Maiden T-shirts from a cart in Glasgow. We were fanned by fruit bats the size of cats, cicadas made a near perfect major fifth with the purring air-con, and the hairdresser poured out a bottle of Château Margaux.

Halfway down the second bottle he began to trust us.

Come here, he said, beckoning.

We ducked through a tunnel made by two kissing bombax trees and came to a shed, painted gold. The hairdresser unlocked several padlocks, touched a mezuzah screwed to the door frame, opened the door, lit a hurricane lamp, and waved us inside.

The shed was carpeted with freshly cut leaves. The walls were bright blue, and, except at the far end, the space was empty. At the far end stood a stone table. On it was an incense burner, and immediately above was a photograph, draped with red and yellow plastic carnations from a Brahmin's wedding.

"Fucking hell," said Nigel.

Well, quite. It was a common swift.

* * *

The photo had been taken a long way upriver. It was blurred and stained. It showed a single bird against the sky, well off the center of the picture, and apparently above a grove of mangroves.

The hairdresser genuflected, lit some joss sticks, genuflected again, and walked backward to the door, pushing us behind him. He fastened the locks in silence, chivvied us back to the courtyard, and topped up our glasses.

The swift wasn't mentioned. We turned to the downside of raw sewage in the bay.

When we left, late that night, Nigel said: "We've got to go there, don't you think? Upriver?"

"I think we should," said I. And so we did.

* * *

Nigel had never knowingly seen a swift, although their screams must have ruffled the water-lily pond of satellite TV dishes that was the roof of his native Lambhill, and he'd never shown any interest in any bird that didn't come in a skirt or with roast potatoes. But now he was a man possessed.

"We can leave at three thirty," he said. "It'll be cool then."

"It won't be cool at all," I replied. "Might as well leave it until six. The heat'll be easing off then."

"In the *morning*, I meant." And he laughed fanatically.

"There's no hurry," I said. "There really isn't."

I said that with complete confidence. I wasn't sure where the confidence came from.

"There are plenty of swifts around," I added.

This, theoretically, was true. It was early September. Oxford swifts should have been passing through on their relatively leisurely return to the deep heart of Africa. But that's not why I'd said there was no hurry.

Nigel wouldn't be contradicted. We left at 3:30 a.m., hungover, unshaven, unbreakfasted, and, on my part, resentful. This wasn't what I'd had in mind at all.

Nigel drove manically through the dawn. We stopped only when a dog died loudly under the front wheels, again so that I could throw up under a baobab, and when the axle snapped.

The axle brought out the best and the worst in the man. He was tyrannically masterful, indefatigable, brutal. My memory insists that he stopped another car, extracted its axle, and left a family of nine weeping in the bush on the side of the road beside their wrecked vehicle. Though that can't be right, it's how it felt. Whatever happened, soon enough (too soon), we were drinking beer by some mangroves, Nigel was scanning the sky with huge naval binoculars, and I was checking the departure times of buses back to the coast.

There weren't any. I had to stay with him and watch him watch. He listened, too, for the swift screech he'd read about, until I told him that common swifts are silent in Africa. That helped: he'd been jumping up whenever a door squeaked or someone trod on a cat.

Usually he paced up and down by the river, stiff-necked, squinting at the sun, expecting swifts to burst out of it. He'd be up as soon as it was light (though swifts are relatively late risers), drinking black coffee to keep his reflexes keen, changing position in case the swifts were hiding behind a tree, sometimes hiding himself and jumping out in case it was some sort of cat-and-mouse game. As the sun set he'd cradle a mournful glass of duty-free Johnnie Walker, watch nightjars, and look cheated.

There was no hurry. They weren't going to come just yet. There was time to watch the postcards curl, and the tree with human fingers form a fist, and the premature patina of decay inch over the thatch. The whole place was waiting for a storm, and had been waiting since the last storm. Waiting is what it did.

Everywhere there were wooden masks with slit eyes, and I don't believe they'd been deconsecrated. We were hundreds of miles inland, but there was a good yard and a half of tide. There was no sign that the sea and the land were negotiating. The sea didn't have to make any concessions at all. Gray-headed gulls fought, like my children with spicy chicken wings, over the bald leg of a Guinea baboon. The head of the femur glistened like a pearl. Big old things with mustaches slunk in the mangrove arches and were sometimes dragged out, not complaining much, clubbed, and overcooked to kill the spearheaded worms that moved in and out of their bowels.

"We're not going until we see them, you know," said Nigel after a few tense days of this.

"Of course not," I said.

The next day we drove out into bristling bush, away from sleek mud and menace. Here little brown things started up and sprang into the blue or into dark thorn tunnels. The only dead things were white and dry. The worst threats are always moist, and so this place, precisely because it didn't throw out its arms in perspiring welcome, was kinder than the river.

I was tired from watching Nigel's watching. I took off my jacket, propped myself against a tree, counted ants, and went to sleep.

I must have slept for half an hour. I slumped sideways. And then, suddenly, I was awake and on my feet, shouting, "They're here, they're here!"

Nigel was fast asleep, too. I kicked him awake. I pointed at the sky. For a moment there was nothing there but a sliver of cloud. And then they were there as I knew they would be, seven of them, screaming silently, straight from Oxford and the throne of heaven, high and then low, hunting the wind, plowing through a thermal that must have been whirring a thousand feet up like the fan on an old bus, trawling a whole weather system because they're birds of the whole world.

"Fucking hell," said Nigel.

Well, quite.

* * *

A beetle caught by a swift over the Pyrenees might still be alive over the Gambia, twitching in the throat pouch, and its carapace might arc down in a mote of dung over a contingent of soldiers in the DRC. The carapace might deflect a bullet aimed at the head of an enemy. You never know. But you don't need a fanciful account of benign causation for swifts to matter.

I can travel the same route as the swift, though not as ecstatically, and not as influentially. I've tried. Their annual migrations, crossing and recrossing the equator, stitch the earth together. They keep the two halves from falling apart. It's practical, surgical *tikkun olam*. When we use violent words for swifts we're describing scalpels and needles. When I cried with Rachel on their return, it was relief that the world was going to hold together for another year.

The other sort of words—ethereal—are really high-priestly. The swifts are doing something on our behalf. Their motion is redemptive. They move constantly so that we don't have to. A badger can be local, living in a hole in a Welsh hill, because there are moving things—supremely the swifts—that do the movement that's necessary. They're the throbbing hearts and tidal chests. They keep the bellows of the world working, enabling slow things to sleep without dying. They keep oxygen bubbling through standing water so that other things can breathe. To be still is to die. Moving things enable stillness: the exuberantly international enables and legitimizes the parochial.

Movement is built into all sustainable systems. God's preference for the mover over the settler is clear and consistent. The shifting pastoralist is better than the static farmer, and the farmer, bitterly envious of his brother's higher status, does his best in all generations to kill him. Cain's doing a good job with the swifts. They're declining fast, killed by the desire of suburban householders to insulate their lofts—to be warmer, safer, more settled. (This reduces swift nesting sites.) If the swifts go, we'll go, too.

It's the people who really can't move who know how much we need the swifts. The iconic human figure in swift literature is the MS sufferer in a motorized wheelchair, looking up at the wheeling swifts inscribing Platonic forms on a summer sky, and saying: "Yes, because they can move, and because I'm part of them, I can move too."

I was woken at the foot of that tree in the West African bush by silent swifts that, at that point, were still a couple of miles away. It was an intimacy greater than I'd known with any of the other species, perhaps precisely because I knew that I could get nowhere near them by sliding or jumping or sailing.

There's a power that comes with total surrender. Perhaps I could fly with the swifts only because I couldn't otherwise move at all with them, or perhaps move at all. Yet the swifts had made Nigel move. Eventually they'll fly him to a frustrated standstill. By then he'll have the habits: he'll be caught up in the net by the scythe-winged fishers of men; he'll be held by the sticky tentacles of entangling Mind; he'll be blissfully plowed in the morphic field and could really start to grow.

* * *

I mustn't make it sound easy. You have to put in the miles.

Not long ago I sat in a hot tepee as a very pretty shaman in a tank top told us how we could meet our spirit animals.

"Relax," she told us. "Close your eyes. Then picture a hole. It could be a rabbit hole, or a fox hole. Anything, really, but ideally going directly into the earth. Then imagine that you're going down into it. Picture it as clearly as you can. See the tree roots. Squirm round them. Smell the leaf mold. Keep going down; always down. You'll meet an animal. Greet it. It'll be glad to see you. It's there to help. This is its domain, so be polite: you're the guest. It'll lead you on; lead you down. Keep following. You'll have adventures. And if you have trouble visualizing a hole, just go down the plug hole in your kitchen. It'll take you to the same place."

She began to beat a drum very fast, like a hamster's pulse.

Outside, people were being doused in gong showers, their chi was being lovingly realigned, and my children were hitting one another with tent mallets. We all dived into our holes. I got six inches down, and my head stuck. It stayed there, sweatily, while the others, it turned out, were having a fine old time soaring, galloping, and trotting through other worlds.

"I met a wolf," one of them breathily told us, when we'd returned to the land of holistic massage and fratricide. "A big gray wolf with white flecks on his neck, and huge blue eyes with a golden core. I didn't want to go with him, but he nudged me on with his nose, and his nose was so warm that I felt comfortable. He let me ride on his back. I sank into it, and then began to feel pinecones underfoot—under *his* feet!"

We obligingly gasped and smiled.

"We—I—went steeply up hill. I could smell deer off to my right, but I wasn't hungry. I'd seen a cave through the trees, with some strange bones buried in the floor. I began to scuffle them out with my forefeet. And then I heard the drum calling me back."

It was, he agreed, a much more intense experience than it had been last year.

Well, I'm sorry, but I don't believe it. I don't say he didn't experience what he described. He was plainly honest and earnest. But this wasn't shamanism, as experienced after arduous and painful apprenticeship; after exhaustion, fasting, and huge doses of fly agaric mushrooms. It wasn't this that they crawled for a mile in the dark along a crack in the rock to find. This wasn't a world on the other side of a veil, but one inside a dreadlocked head. It's just not so easy; you have to to acquire the habit: you have to do the legwork, or the wingwork. It's not just about rightly directed imagination or good intention.

The Jewish prayer that's said on first awaking declares that "all who fulfill His commandments gain good understanding." You don't start by understanding: you don't start with an idea. In the beginning was the deed. In a material world—a world of earth, air, fire, and water, with which magical alchemy can be done—you can't grasp abstractions or ghosts direct, as they were trying to do in the tepee. They're too slippery, too insubstantial, too contingent on glorious concreteness. You've got to get dirty in the earth, cold and fearful in the air, singed in the fire, and seasick in the water. You've got to scratch, scratch, scratch the world with the same paw or wing movements as the creatures you long to know.

Swifts have the habit of flying. You've got to get the habit of the swift in order to fly.

EPILOGUE

"So: what's this book about, then?"

I was sitting on an island with a well-known Greek poet who hurrumphed dismissively into his mustache between glasses of Peloponnesian red.

I told him what I thought it was about.

"Impossible." He meant *absurd*, but was too gracious to say so. "It's like trying to live in a fifth dimension. You can describe it mathematically, but you can't give any account of what it would be like to live in it."

"No," I said, "it's not like that. Or if it is, then it makes me doubt whether I have any real human relationships. I'm in the same three spatial dimensions as a fox, and the fourth dimension, time, flows just as mysteriously and erratically for other humans as it does for foxes. True, foxes might get several years' worth of information in a momentary sniff—so telescoping time. But that's not unimaginably different in kind from me flicking quickly through a family photo album."

The poet raised his eyebrows and looked pityingly sophisticated.

I went on, but I didn't know why: "You've got a nose. It's so much more fastidious than the average—and certainly than mine—that you've brought your own bottle of wine with you to this perfectly nice taverna. Yet I can have some idea of what you mean by wine: and even by 'good wine,' and even by some of the adjectives you'd use to describe good wine. And even if I can't now, I could learn. I could awaken my nose."

"But," said he, "I can't have the first idea what it's like to live in the world of a Southern Baptist from Alabama. You can't reeducate your psyche to know anything at all about that."

I agreed with him. That is indeed the world of the fifth or sixth or seventh dimension. But the comparison gave me hope.

"Quite right," I said. "I share much more with a fox than with a fundamentalist. I've lived, and I live, with the fox in an embodied, sensual world of wood and earth and bone and semen and cold. We met and we meet in a real place, and there I've started to use the words *I* and *thou*. The *I* has grown in the encounters, I can tell you. And if the *I* has grown, why not the *thou*? If we grow in the same soil, and in the light beaming from the other, isn't that a sort of knowledge of the other?"

He rolled his eyes, took another swig of the unapproachably, incomprehensibly good wine, and turned to the accents of Cretans and Thracians.

The taverna looked out onto an olive grove where, in happier, wiser times, cloven-footed Pan had serenaded and impregnated the maidens of Kythira. Like any decent or indecent maenad I drank the wine made from the grapes just down the road, and eventually the premise of the book didn't seem so ludicrous. I thought it was fair, if not encouraging, to judge it by its fruits.

* * *

I grew up on the edge. On the edge of a community (we never really belonged anywhere), and on the seam of a city and the wilderness. At night I'd walk up a few polite streets and then the neon would give up and I'd be looking down at the city: one foot on the heather, another on the asphalt; one foot in the light, another in the dark.

Those night walks defined me. I was made by the edges. Take them away and I'd dissolve. I couldn't survive on either the heather or the asphalt.

I wondered whether other people were the same. I still wonder. Selfishly I hope so. I'd like to meet them.

I grew up, therefore, both suspicious of frontiers and totally dependent on them. Then, after a bit of wandering and reading, I wondered whether humans could cross the frontiers that separate them from other species. Those frontiers seemed pretty artificial—defined by the taxonomical conventions of the day. And by all accounts they had been routinely violated (as the Judeo-Christian tradition, with its love of separation, would put it), or rapturously and enrichingly penetrated (as shaggy people who played the pipes and seemed to have more fun would put it) in most cultures other than our own.

I could have gone down the stern, merry, green path of the shaman. But I was too scared. Instead I took up bird-watching and philosophical abstraction.

As far as the abstraction goes, I'm interested in three questions. Although it might not have been obvious, I've been exploring them in this book.

The first flows directly from heather, asphalt, and shamanism: Are there any limits to our ability to choose?

The fact that we have at least some autonomy is awesome and intimidating. We're used to thinking that autonomy is most critically on trial in dramatic, occasional situations—such as when we're considering the right to assisted suicide. But surely it's the day-to-day choices that are the most terrifying and repercussive. Listen: you can choose whether to get up early, run around a field, have a cold bath, and then read

Middlemarch. Or stay in bed and watch shopping TV. That's astonishing. I can never get over it. That's a choice between life and death. Therefore choose life.

We're used to saying, at least to ourselves, "There's nothing I can't do or be if I put my mind to it." But is it true?

There's a good test for this. If I can become a badger, then there are good reasons to be confident more generally about our autonomy.

The second question has to do with identity and authenticity.

I've often worried that there's nothing to me. Or at least that, if there is something to me, it's highly labile. I would like to be reassured that there's an indestructible core of Charles-Fosterishness.

One way of testing this is by becoming a fox, and seeing if the fox still smells distinctively like me.

The third question relates to otherness.

I worry that I'm entirely alone in the world: that otherness is wholly inaccessible. That when I think I'm in a relationship, I'm not. That all conversations are ultimately at cross-purposes. That I neither understand nor am understood by any other.

There's an exercise that might be able to help. If I can establish a real relationship with a nonhuman animal, there are grounds for optimism with regard to relationships with humans. If I can bond with a swift, I may well be able to bond with my children. True, I won't be able to prove in a Euclidean sort of way that I'm really relating to the swift. But the human-animal relationship will be simpler than the human-human one, and it won't be obscured by so much tangled emotion. That means it might be easier to be reassured that a human-animal relationship is real. If it is, and it tastes like the same sort of thing as a human-human relationship, I'll be able to love my children less doubtfully.

These are what I was working on in the mountains, moors, rivers, seas, and skies.

I made, I think, a bit of progress.

Our anatomy and physiology impose some limits on us. And if (as seems highly unlikely) we're mortal, so does our mortality. I can't fly. Nor is there time to learn all the words necessary to compensate poetically for my absence of wings. But our capacity for vicariousness is infinite. Empathize enough with a swift and you'll either become one or (which may be the same thing) you'll be able to rejoice so much with the screeching race around the church tower that you won't mind not being one yourself.

For better or for worse, Charles Foster continued to smell of himself when he crawled, slashed, and dived. Indeed he smelled *more* like himself. That wasn't, I think, because the whole exercise of transformation was a failure, but rather it was an illustration of the general principle that the more you give away, the more you get back. In any event, it was reassuring. There's *something* in me that's distinctive and worth working on.

I've seen and known some animal others. The woods are full of slinking *thou*s! I've been held in a yard in the East End of London by the commanding vertical pupil of an insolent fox. I've had enough beckoning and threatening looks across crowded bars to know reciprocity and its absence when I see them.

This is immensely exciting. There's a chance that I can know and be known!

* * *

There was a fourth less abstract question. Do my animals live in the same world as I do? Do they swim in the same water, forage in the same garbage cans, dig in the same earth, look across the same misty Channel to Wales, and smell the same rising tide of decay from the Gulf of Guinea?

I've left it until last because my thoughts about it change about every half an hour, and I hoped for a while that they would start to crystallize.

They haven't, and I'm so glad.

* * *

I can't always be in the wild. Sometimes I have to be in places that smell of fear, fumes, and ambition. When I'm there, it helps very much to know that badgers are asleep inside a Welsh hill, that an otter is turning over stones in one of the Rockford pools, that a fox is blinking in the same sun that makes me sweat in my tweed coat, that a red stag is cudding among ghost trees by a stone circle near Hoar Oak, and that there's a swift, hatched above my Oxford study, hunting, almost beyond human sight, in the high hot blue over the Congo River.

That these things should be a comfort is strange. They should taunt, not comfort. They should say: "You're not there. Ha, ha, ha."

Why does that not happen?

Well, I note that I get a similar sense of comfort only from being assured of the continued existence of things—and notably people—that (whatever love is) I love.

Perhaps, then (whatever love means), I *love* these creatures. I cringe at the thought. For the last two hundred pages I've been terrified of anthropomorphism, and here I am, apparently guilty of the very worst kind.

It gets worse. Because the sort of love I'm talking about (whatever it is) is necessarily reciprocal. I can't really love X unless X loves me.

Now there's a thought.

ACKNOWLEDGMENTS
AND BIBLIOGRAPHY

Bibliographies and acknowledgments are usually separate. I think that's strange. There's no clear distinction between a person and the books they've read. If I ask someone for an opinion or for information, their answer will draw on a mass of literature. Here, then, people and paper are in the same place.

This is not a full list of everyone who's helped. A full list would be everyone I've ever met, seen, and heard, and everyone who has met, seen, and heard them, and so on in an infinite regression.

I have changed some names.

The bibliography is very selective. It contains just the basic texts that might be useful for anyone who wants to read more. I read hundreds of scientific papers when researching this book. Only five of them are cited here: about badger predation by wolves, because lots of people didn't believe the account in the chapter; about empathy in animals, because the subject is particularly controversial, and the paper surveys all the crucial studies; about ranging behavior in red deer, from which I borrowed many facts; about the physiological responses of red deer to being hunted (because the issue is discussed in this book, and the cited article supplements the Bateson Report and the Joint Universities Study, both of which are separately cited here); and about swift migration, because I have used much of the data from it in the swift chapter.

GENERAL

People

My wonderful friends Jay Griffiths and Iain McGilchrist, who believed in this book when there was no reason at all to do so. I wrote the first words sitting in Iain's house on Skye, looking out at a storm mounting over the Uists, as Iain shucked oysters for supper. And I drafted the final words in my head as I walked with Jay over Brendon Common on Exmoor, having just been hunted by bloodhounds.

My amazing agent, Jessica Woollard; my superb editors, Mike Jones and Rebecca Gray at Profile and Riva Hocherman at Metropolitan; Juliana Froggat and Emily DeHuff for scarily acute copyediting; and kind, wise George Lucas at Inkwell Management.

Colin Roberts, for all that happy, formative anarchy in the Peak District, and Derek Whiteley and Andy Powell for infecting me with a passion for natural history from which I'll never recover.

Mark and Sue West of Indicknowle Farm, Combe Martin, for affirming my identity as Badger Man.

Nigel and Janet Phillips, the best two things I've ever picked up on a beach.

For all sorts of things: Paul Kingsnorth, Andy Letcher, Hugh Warwick, James Crowden, Arita Baaijens, David Bostock, Geoff and Mandy Johnson, Katherine Stathatos, Gus Greenlees, Annabel Foulger, Magnus Boyd, Marnie Buchanan,

Karl Segnoe, the *Dark Mountain* lot, and the editors of *Shooting Times* (UK).

My long-suffering wife, Mary.

And of course the cubs/calves/nestlings: Lizzie, Sally, Tom, Jamie, Rachel, and Jonny, who are far and away my most important teachers.

1. Becoming a Beast

Abram, David. *Becoming Animal: An Earthly Cosmology*. Pantheon, 2010.

———. *The Spell of the Sensuous: Perception and Language in a More-Than-Human World*. Vintage, 1997.

Griffiths, Jay. *Wild: An Elemental Journey*. Penguin, 2007.

Bradbury, Jack, and Sandra L. Vehrencamp. *Principles of Animal Communication*. Sinauer, 2011.

Klein, Bradley G. *Cunningham's Textbook of Veterinary Physiology*. Saunders, 2012.

Morell, Virginia. *Animal Wise: The Thoughts and Emotions of Our Fellow Creatures*. Old Street Publishing, 2013.

Household, Geoffrey. *Rogue Male*. Chatto and Windus, 1939.

Rothenberg, David. *Survival of the Beautiful: Art, Science and Evolution*. Bloomsbury, 2011.

Lewis-Williams, David, and David Pearce. *Inside the Neolithic Mind: Consciousness, Cosmos and the Realm of the Gods*. Thames and Hudson, 2009.

McGilchrist, Iain. *The Master and His Emissary: The Divided Brain and the Making of the Western World*. Yale University Press, 2012.

Monbiot, George. *Feral: Rewilding the Land, Sea and Human Life*. Penguin, 2014.

Baker, J. A., introduction by Robert Macfarlane. *The Peregrine*. New York Review of Books Classics, 2005.

Foer, Jonathan Safran. *Eating Animals*. Hamish Hamilton, 2009.

"B.B" [Denys James Watkins-Pitchford]. *Brendon Chase*. Hollis, 1944.

2. BADGER

People

Burt and Meg, of course
Dr. Chris Newman, WildCRU, University of Oxford
Derek Gow, Upcott Grange Farm
Hugh Warwick
Mark West, Indicknowle Farm
Many of the volunteers at Wytham Woods, Oxford

Books

Neal, Ernest. *The Badger*. Collins, 1969.
Roper, Tim. *Badger*. Collins, 2010.
Clark, Michael. *Badgers*. Whittet, 2010.
Barkham, Patrick. *Badgerlands: The Twilight World of Britain's Most Enigmatic Animal*. Granta, 2013.
Justice, Daniel Heath. *Badger*. Reaktion, 2015.
Jones, Cynan. *The Dig*. Granta, 2014.

Article

Sidorovich, V. E., I. I. Rotenko, and D. A. Krasko, "Badger *Meles meles* spatial structure and diet in an area of low earthworm biomass and high predator risk," *Annales Zoologici Fennici* 48, no. 1 (2011): 1–16.

3. OTTER

People

Nigel Phillips, Somerset Wildlife Trust
Ione Willcock, Exmoor National Park Authority
Simon, James, Richard, and Wendy Wyburn, Staghunters' Inn, Brendon, Exmoor

Books

Allen, Daniel. *Otter*. Reaktion, 2010.
Darlington, Miriam. *Otter Country: In Search of the Wild Otter*. Granta, 2012.

Chanin, Paul, and Guy Troughton. *Otters*. Whittet, 2013.

Kruuk, Hans. *Otters: Ecology, Behaviour and Conservation*. Oxford University Press, 2006.

Williams, James. *The Otter*. Merlin Unwin, 2010.

Williamson, Henry. *Tarka the Otter*. G. P. Putnam's Sons, 1927.

Maxwell, Gavin. *Raven Seek Thy Brother*. Longmans, 1969.

———. *Ring of Bright Water*. Longmans, 1960.

———. *The Rocks Remain*. Longmans, 1963.

4. FOX

People

Professor David Macdonald, WildCRU, University of Oxford

The Joint Masters at the time of the Coniston Foxhounds, the Blencathra Foxhounds, the Lunesdale Foxhounds, the Melbreak Foxhounds, the Pennine Foxhounds, the Dumfriesshire Foxhounds, the South Shropshire Foxhounds and (though they don't hunt foxes) the Ecclesfield Beagles, the Shropshire Beagles, and the Trinity Foot Beagles

Several sheep farmers in the High Peak, Derbyshire

Roger and Doreen Westmoreland

Malcolm and Pip Chisholm

Mike Smith

Mervyn Vickery

Books

Henry, J. David. *Red Fox: The Cat-like Canine:* Smithsonian Books, 1996.

Macdonald, David. *Running with the Fox*. HarperCollins, 1989.

Harris, Stephen. *Urban Foxes*. Whittet, 2001.

Wallen, Martin. *Fox*. Reaktion, 2006.

Lloyd, H. G. *The Red Fox*. Batsford, 1980.

"B.B." [Denys James Watkins-Pitchford]. *Wild Lone: The Story of a Pytchley Fox*. Eyre and Spottiswoode, 1938.

Bradshaw, John. *In Defense of Dogs*. Penguin, 2012.

5. RED DEER

People

Dr. John Fletcher, Reedie Hill Deer Farm, Auchtermuchty
Richard Eales, Exmoor National Park Authority
David Greenwood, Joint Master of the Devon and Somerset Stag-
hounds
The Joint Masters at the time of the Devon and Somerset Stag-
hounds, the Quantock Staghounds, and the Tiverton Staghounds
Many stalkers and ghillies across the Scottish Highlands
Duff and Phylla Hart-Davies
David Lyon
Katy Stewart-Smith
Dr. Chris Thouless, Save the Elephants
Dr. Murray Corke, Department of Clinical Veterinary Medicine,
University of Cambridge
Professor Peter Clegg, School of Veterinary Science, University of
Liverpool
Professor Roger Smith, Royal Veterinary College
Professor Christine Nicol, School of Veterinary Sciences, University
of Bristol
Dr. Liz Paul, School of Veterinary Sciences, University of Bristol
Dr. Jo Edgar, School of Veterinary Sciences, University of Bristol
Matthew Price
Farlap Bloodhounds

Books, Chapters, Reports

Jefferies, Richard. *Red Deer*. Longmans, Green, 1884.
Williamson, Henry. "Stumberleap." In *The Old Stag*. G. P. Putnam's
Sons, 1926.
Fortescue, J. W. *The Story of a Red Deer*. Sportsman's Press, 1897.
Fletcher, John. *Deer*. Reaktion, 2013.
Hart-Davies, Duff. *Monarchs of the Glen: A History of Deer Stalking
in the Scottish Highlands*. Jonathan Cape, 1978.
———. *Among the Deer*. Quiller Press, 2011.
Prior, Richard. *Deer Watch*. Swan Hill, 2007.

Chalmers, Patrick. *Mine Eyes to the Hills: An Anthology of the Highland Forest.* A. C. Black, 1931.

Langbein, Jochen, and Rory Putman. "Studies of English red deer populations subject to hunting-to-hounds," chapter 12 in *The Exploitation of Mammal Populations,* edited by Victoria J. Taylor and Nigel Dunstone. Chapman and Hall, 1996.

Bateson, P. *The behavioural and physiological effects of culling red deer.* Report to the National Trust, London, 1997.

Harris, R. C., T. R. Helliwell, W. Shingleton, N. Stickland, and J.R.J. Naylor. *The physiological response of red deer (*Cervus elaphus*) to prolonged exercise undertaken during hunting.* Newmarket: R&W Publications, 1999.

Articles

Edgar, J. L., C. J. Nicol, C.C.A. Clark, and E. S. Paul. "Measuring empathic responses in animals." *Applied Animal Behaviour Science* 138 (2012): 182–93.

Langbein, Jochen. "The ranging behaviour, habitat-use and impact of deer in oak woods and heather moors on Exmoor." *Deer* 10 (1997): 516–21.

Thomas, L. H., and W. R. Allen. "A Veterinary Opinion on Hunting with Hounds." http://www.vet-wildlifemanagement.org.uk /images/stories/item-images/pdf/VetOpinion.pdf.

6. SWIFT

People

Professor Tim Birkhead, University of Sheffield

Professor Susanne Akesson, Lund University

Dr. Andrew Gosler, Edward Grey Institute, University of Oxford

Professor Yossi Leshem, Tel Aviv University

Amnonn Hahn

Shira Twersky-Cassell

All at the International Common Swift Seminars, and particularly Ulrich Tigges, Chris Mason, and Gillian Westray

Books

Lack, David. *Swifts in a Tower*. Methuen, 1956.

Chantler, Phil, and Gerald Driessens. *Swifts: A Guide to the Swifts and Tree-swifts of the World*. Pica, 2000.

Sheldrake, Rupert. *Dogs That Know When Their Owners Are Coming Home: And Other Unexplained Powers of Animals*. Arrow, 2000.

———. *The Presence of the Past: Morphic Resonance and the Habits of Nature*. Icon, 2011.

Garner, Alan. *Boneland*. Fourth Estate, 2012.

Article

Åkesson, S. R. Klaassen, J. Holmgren, J. W. Fox, and A. Hedenström. "Migration Routes and Strategies in a Highly Aerial Migrant, the Common Swift *Apus apus*, Revealed by Light-Level Geolocators." PLOS ONE 7(7) e41195 (2012), doi: 10.1371/journal/pone.0041195.

INDEX